TWIN CITIES
HAUNTED HANDBOOK

AMERICA'S
HAUNTED ROAD TRIP

TWIN CITIES
HAUNTED HANDBOOK

Jeff Morris

Garett Merk

Dain Charbonneau

clerisy press

Twin Cities Haunted Handbook

For further information, contact the publisher at:
   Clerisy Press
   306 Greenup Street
   Covington, Kentucky 41011
   www.clerisypress.com

Cataloging-in-Publication Data is available from the Library of Congress

ISBN 978-1-57860-507-1

Distributed by Publishers Group West
Printed in the United States of America
First edition, first printing

Editor: Donna Poehner
Cover design by Scott McGrew
Text design by Annie Long
Cover and interior photos provided by the authors unless otherwise noted.

CONTENTS

SECTION I   parks and lakes   3

SECTION II cemeteries, hospitals, and churches   49

ACKNOWLEDGMENTS

WE WOULD LIKE TO START BY THANKING all of those nameless people out there who made this book possible. During our countless hours of research into this vast array of haunted locations, so many people helped us who either wished to remain anonymous or whose name we never knew. It almost seems unfair that many of those people who have helped us out the most may not be individually mentioned in this section. For this reason, we feel that these people should be mentioned first. You have our most sincere apology for not mentioning your name, and you have our most sincere thank you.

Next, there are a handful of people who helped us with the daunting amount of research that was necessary for this book. Without these people, this book would not have been possible: Beth Fontaine, Chad Brinkley, Nicole Dunn, Tiffany Long, Jerry Zoeller, Matt Kroeger, Michael Lamping, and Richard Miller. I would also like to thank a couple of groups that aided us along the way. Anoka County Historical Society, Para Adventures, Twin Cities Paranormal Research Group.

Many individual stories throughout this book can be credited to individuals who helped us to find the stories and histories of the locations. A handful of locations on the east side of the Twin Cities were attained with the help of the Hastings Paranormal Team and Dakota County Paranormal Society. Without them, locations such as the St. James Hotel, Hastings State Asylum Cemetery, The Onion Grille, and several others would not have been possible.

Another person who helped us during Garett and Jeff's long trip to Minnesota was Ryan Vehr. Ryan spent his own time and money for little credit. He simply wanted to join us in the adventure that has become this book.

Finally, we would all like to extend individual thanks to family and to people who have helped us:

DAIN—I would like to thank my dad for sharing his interests and insights into the paranormal and joining me occasionally on trips to many of the locations. I'd like to thank my mother for always supporting and encouraging me throughout my entire life. I thank Steven and Juliet for their willingness to always loan me their equipment on many of my outings. I also would like to acknowledge Dan, Nicole, Reane, Tammy, Marcus, Isabel, Grace, Austin, Oliver, Zoey, Scarlet, Jilena, and Steph. Thanks to the folks over at Real Ghost Tours for the wonderful experience they provide at St. Anthony Main. I'd also like to extend a special thanks to Elaine for her love and support throughout this entire endeavor.

JEFF—I can't express my gratitude enough towards everyone in my life who has encouraged and supported me through the creation of this book. Amy, Koen, and Koda, my family, have allowed me the necessary time to both work on the book at home and travel to Minnesota for research. My parents have also been generous and supportive during the writing of this book, and they also deserve my most sincere thanks.

GARETT—To start, I'd like to thank God and my parents for making me; if they hadn't done that, I wouldn't be able to help write this book. I'd also like to thank Paul Bunyan's blue ox, Babe, for stepping all over the land to make the many, many lakes throughout the Twin Cities. I'd also like to give credit to Ryan, Jerry, Mike, Matt, Mark, Bob, Terry, Joe, Sterling, and Garfield. A huge thank-you to Jeff's car for not dying on our trip to the Twin Cities—you done good, car.

FOREWORD

A MONSTER LIVES IN MY BEDROOM CLOSET. The closet itself sits slightly ajar on the wall closest to my side of the bed. I use it for storage. Remnants of my past are boxed and stacked within the small space: report cards and photographs from grade school and high school, souvenirs from summer vacations to Civil War battlefields, a photograph of someone I used to know by a fountain that I no longer recognize, a shard of wood from an old amusement park I wrote about in my first book but that no longer exists except in memory, yellowing pages of a short story I wrote in college about a coded treasure map that held a secret I no longer remember, tangible memories of my past that I never look at but know are there.

The monster has yellow eyes. At night, I'll sometimes awake from some interesting nightmare and look over towards the closet. Since my eyes have not yet become accustomed to the pitch darkness of the room, all I can see are the thin ovals of the monster's yellowish glowing eyes as it peers out at me.

Some say that fear is biological and measurable. When one is frightened, certain things happen within his or her body. Adrenaline begins to flow. Eyes dilate to take in more light. Hearts beat faster to give muscles more fuel to fight or flee. Other senses are enhanced. One's body places itself upon the precipice of action. So why are we so often frozen in fear? Why, despite our body preparing us for confrontation, are we so often frozen in inaction.

Fear is often directed towards the unknown. We cannot act against something we do not understand. All I know about my monster is that it lives in the closet and it has yellow eyes. I don't know the color of its skin. I don't know the size of its teeth or its claws. All I know is it watches me silently throughout the night with those piercing yellow eyes.

The ultimate unknown is death. Sure, we struggle to escape the maniacal serial killer or the bloodthirsty creatures that may chase us in the night, but what we fear most is what will happen when they catch us. We know that they will kill us. We know that we will die. What we don't know is where we will be after we die. Will we wander the earth as a spirit, never completely grasping who we are or in what stage of existence we are trapped? Is there a heaven? Is there a hell?

I've heard people refer to those of us who go headlong into haunted places looking for evidence of ghosts as brave. They claim that they would be too frightened if they were to ever actually encounter a ghost. They respect the bravery of those who seem to actually want to find a ghost. I would suggest though that instead of bravery, there is also a degree of cowardice that drives me towards these ghosts. As I've said, fear seems to follow the unknown. If I were to find these ghosts and ultimately understand them, the mystery around them will dissipate. If ghosts are in fact remnants of people who have died, this will also ease my own fears of death.

The more people looking for these answers, the higher the probability that someone will find them.

This philosophy is constantly in the subconscious part of my brain. Thinking about it now, it seems that this is somewhat an inspiration for the Haunted Handbook series. These books are essentially travel books. They tell you the history and the ghost stories of the haunted locations in the subject city, but perhaps just as importantly, they tell you how to get to the places and how to look for the ghosts there. The more people out there and the more haunted locations they are exploring, the higher the chances are that people will find that key piece of evidence that gives them another clue as to what is really out there. With this knowledge or even the desire to pursue this knowledge, the fear begins to disappear. Fear is replaced with curiosity and thirst for understanding.

Each book in the Haunted Handbook series has at least 100 haunted locations. These locations are all within about an hour of the subject city. This makes it incredibly easy for anyone who lives in these cities or is visiting these cities to look for these ghosts. This makes the locations accessible. Accessibility was always the thing that I felt was lacking in other books on ghosts. These other books had great stories, but the places were hidden or too far away to go visit. Accessibility is important because, although the ghost stories and the histories of these places are fascinating in and of themselves, there are those of us who like to go out and find out for ourselves what's really out there. We need to see in order to believe.

I know the monster is in my closet because I've seen its yellow eyes. My wife hasn't seen it, so she thinks I'm making it up.

While finding answers to the issues that frighten us is important, it is also important to understand the path we took to get to where we are. History is important. Ghosts and ghost stories are like a piece of history themselves. These ghosts tell the story of what happened in a place. Ghosts tell the story of past mistakes. In almost all instances, ghosts cannot hurt you. They scare you because you don't fully understand where they came from or what they are.

Working on the books in this series has taught me a lot. I know more about the subject cities and have learned more about Minneapolis and St. Paul than I ever imagined was possible. I know things about the history behind certain locations that some people who have lived near those places all their lives don't know. Sometimes, this history is hidden in some metaphorical dark recess and only the dead can tell us what once happened there.

Don't be afraid of the ghosts. They can be scary. They can jump out at you. They can be strange. They can be deformed and creepy. You can hear them sometimes, or see them, or simply feel them.

When I die, I will leave behind a history. I don't know for sure if I will return as a ghost. If I do, you can learn about me and my past through my own spirit. I promise I will do my best to come back and haunt those of you who would like to be haunted. If I don't come back as a ghost though, I still have a tangible collection of souvenirs from my past, a tangible collection of history that simply needs to be collected and documented, so it is not lost to the destructiveness of time. That history is in my closet, guarded by a monster with yellow eyes.

HAPPY GHOSTING!

—*Jeff Morris*

INTRODUCTION

UNLIKE MY CO-AUTHORS, I am by no means a hardcore ghost hunter; I hunt on a much more casual level. I do not carry around and set up every piece of ghost hunting equipment under the sun, nor do I spend hours to days reviewing the evidence I have gathered. But with that said, I greatly enjoy experiencing the thrill of the "hunt." From a young age, I always experienced excitement in visiting places with stories of being haunted. I start by digging into and understanding the history of a place and then review the reported paranormal activity. Finally, I physically go to the location to investigate. When I visit a location, I do not go out of my way to try to prove a thing many will never accept and the rest may never fully understand; but rather my goal is to disprove the paranormal activity. I feel that if paranormal activity cannot be disproved, then you have something truly interesting.

This book will provide you with 100 locations around the Twin Cities where there have been claims of paranormal activity. We want this book to be for those in the Twin Cities, so we have ensured that all 100 locations are within about an hour's drive of downtown Minneapolis or St. Paul. Many of these locations have rich histories few know about but that help can help you understand the paranormal activity. This book will give you the historical information that may be tied to paranormal activity. Unlike other ghost books, this book has done some legwork for those looking for more than just information about locations with paranormal activity. Each location has driving directions, hours it's open to the public to visit, and the times we feel would be best to experience paranormal activity. The rest we leave up to you, so you can draw your own conclusions as to whether a location has paranormal activity.

Whether you are seeking to investigate the paranormal, hoping to validate the paranormal, looking to debunk the paranormal, seeking a paranormal experience, or just looking to visit the locations in this book for the extra thrill, I wish you Happy Hunting!

—*Dain*

Rules for Exploring the Locations in this Book

WHAT FOLLOWS ARE NOT GUIDELINES but indispensable rules you must follow at all costs. As ghost hunters, we have certain responsibilities. We are not lawbreakers. We are not vandals. We are researchers. We are curious. We are archaeologists and scientists. We are adventurers.

1)   Keep your own safety in mind at all times: Many of the locations can be dangerous if not approached cautiously. After all, many of the ghosts encountered in the book have died from accidents in these very locations. Some places aren't in the best of neighborhoods where you shouldn't go alone at night with expensive equipment. Some places are along dangerous roads or in dangerous parks. Nothing is worth putting your own life in jeopardy. Be smart. Take a friend. Let people know where you are going. Do not put yourself into harm's way.

2)   Obey the law: Listed in many of the following chapters are guidelines for visiting the haunted locations. Some cemeteries are open throughout the night, while others close at dark. If you enter cemeteries, businesses, or parks after they are closed, you are trespassing, and saying that you're "looking for ghosts" will not save you from being arrested. Also, the guidelines that I mentioned are always subject to change. Cemeteries, parks, or businesses may change their hours of operation or their rules. If posted signs at the location give hours or rules different than the ones listed in this book, follow the information on the signs posted at the location.

3)   Show respect: Many of the following locations are deeply imbedded with historical significance. Do not disrespect the memory of those who once walked here. As ghost hunters, we need to create a reputation as people who respect history and the places where the dead may still roam. If we gain a reputation as people who destroy historical landmarks or who act like children, it will make it harder to gain access to any haunted location in the future. These ghosts trying so hard to be heard may be forced to suffer in perpetual silence.

The authors of this book cannot take responsibility for those who disregard these rules. This book is meant to encourage people to learn about and even experience the ghosts and history of the Twin Cities, not to hurt anyone or upset the community. Keep your adventures legal, respectful, and, above all, keep them safe.

HAPPY GHOSTING!

SECTION I

parks and lakes

ADAM'S HILL PARK

7200 Washburn Avenue, Richfield, Minnesota 55423

directions

Take I-35W South from downtown Minneapolis for 7 miles until you reach exit 9C, the 76th Street exit. At the end of the exit ramp, turn right onto 76th Street and follow that for about half a mile before turning right onto Penn Avenue South. Follow Penn Avenue for another half mile and then turn left onto West 72nd Street, which will take you straight onto Washburn Avenue and into Adam's Hill Park.

history

Until around 1981, there was nothing desirable about the land on and around Adam's Hill. The land surrounding the small hill was quite marshy. Whenever it rained, the area would essentially become a swamp, and the water would spread into surrounding areas, making large areas almost uninhabitable.

In the late 1800s or early 1900s, this surrounding area was used as farmland by a farmer who lived alone. Not only was the farmer alone, but often he was unable to cultivate his crops because of the way the area collected rainwater. Convinced that his own mere survival and happiness were impossible, the farmer decided to commit suicide. He carefully tied a noose from a tree near the bottom of Adam's Hill and hung himself. It was weeks before anyone found the body.

In 1981, the area was redeveloped, and a large holding pond and pump system now redirects the excess rainwater to make the area a pleasant park. According to rumors, the tree where the farmer hung himself still stands near the foot of the hill within the park.

ghost story

The farmer who hung himself in what is today Adam's Hill Park supposedly still roams these grounds. Most commonly, people report seeing the apparition of the farmer walking through the park after dark. He is dressed as a farmer and slowly walks through the park, apparently paying no attention to his surroundings. If he is ever approached, he will slowly fade into the darkness and completely vanish.

People also hear what sound like footsteps falling slowly behind them. When they turn to see who is following them, there is no one there. Other times, people are overcome with feelings of depression and despair while in the park. According to the stories, these feelings are most poignant when they are close to the tree where the farmer hung himself. Another story tells about a tree at the foot of the hill, again supposedly the same tree from which the farmer hung himself, which rustles and shakes even when there is no breeze or animals in the tree.

visiting

The best time to visit Adam's Hill Park with the intention of finding ghosts is after dark. The park is open until 10 p.m. every night. Not only is the apparition of the farmer seen most often after dark, but the park is less busy after dark, and you have much more seclusion and privacy to explore the paranormal side of this place.

ALIMAGNETPARK TRAILS

1200 Alimagnet Parkway, Burnsville, Minnesota 55337

directions

From downtown St. Paul, take I-35E South for about 16.5 miles to exit 90, the CR-11 exit. Turn left to take CR-11 South. After about half a mile, continue to follow CR-11 South by turning right onto McAndrews Road East. After another half mile, turn left to continue following CR-11. After another mile, turn left onto Alimagnet Parkway. Follow Alimagnet Parkway all the way into the park until you get to the lake. The haunted trails cut through the woods adjacent to the lake.

history

Some of the trails near the lake are steep and difficult to traverse. Others are straight and easily navigated. The trails are all confined inside of a park named Alimagnet Park, which was created along the southern shore of the lake. Since the lake is about halfway between Apple Valley and Burnsville, there are actually two different parks. The largest park is the Burnsville Alimagnet Park, and the smaller one is called the

Apple Valley Alimagnet Lake Park. The Burnsville Park takes up the southwestern shore of the lake while the Apple Valley Park takes up the southeast corner.

The strange name of the lake traces its origin to a mishmash of names that were put together by the surveyors who discovered the lake. The surveyors named the lake after three 12-year-old girls they both knew: Alice McQuillen, Margaret Davis, and Nettie Judd. Before European settlers discovered the lake, the lakeshore was frequented by Native American tribes from the area. No one is sure what caused the trails to become haunted, but people typically assume the ghosts have something to do with the Native Americans who once lived here.

ghost story

At the Alimagnet Park Trails, the ghosts seem to wait until the sun sets to come out. The ghosts seem to have one goal: to scare anyone away who walks these trails after the sun has set.

Most of the ghost sightings involve dark, shadowy figures that traverse the trails at night. Witnesses see a figure slowly cross the trail in front of them and then disappear into the pitch darkness of the woods beside the trail. These figures are well known throughout the area, and paranormal groups have gone to the trails at night and have actually witnessed and photographed the phenomenon. Perhaps these shadowy figures are the spirits of Native Americans who are to this day protecting their land.

One particularly strange story has circulated about a ghost seen on these trails. This ghost is seen most often just as the sun is beginning to set, when people walking the trails see a figure in the woods next to the trail. The figure looks like a clown and simply stares at the witnesses from the woods. Onlookers always flee.

visiting

There is nothing preventing you from walking the trails at night, but if you do, make sure you take proper precautions. Some of the trails are somewhat hazardous, and there are some steep slopes near the lakeshore. Make sure you have proper lighting so that you are not injured on the trails.

Many of the witnesses to the shadowy figures are unable to properly document the phenomenon when it occurs. They don't have lights bright enough or cameras that can operate in the darkness well enough. If you are hoping to catch that elusive piece of evidence that proves these trails are actually haunted, bring equipment that allows you to photograph clearly in darkness.

ARCOLA TRAIL BRIDGE

11934 Arcola Trail North, Stillwater, Minnesota 55082

directions

From St. Paul, take I-35E North for about 4 miles to exit 111A, MN-36 East towards Stillwater. Follow MN-36 East for almost 12 miles before turning left onto Manning Avenue North. Follow Manning for about 3 miles and then turn right onto Dellwood Road North. After another mile and a half, turn left onto Stonebridge Trail North. After another 3.5 miles, turn right onto Partridge Road North and then make an immediate left onto St. Croix Trail North. Follow St. Croix Trail North for a little more than 2 miles and then turn right onto Arcola Trail North. The bridge is a railroad bridge a little more than a mile down the road that passes over Arcola Trail North.

history

The Arcola Trail Bridge is an old railroad bridge that crosses over the St. Croix River. The bridge itself has become a fascination for many of the locals. People have called it the "High Bridge" (while this title may seem facetious because of its low clearance from Arcola Trail, it means that it spans high over the St. Croix River) to accentuate the danger of the bridge to pedestrians.

Throughout its history, several people have been killed while walking on the bridge. To this day the bridge is still an operating railroad bridge and has no railings. Many people have walked out onto the bridge for the views, thinking that the tracks looked too old and dilapidated to still be in use, and have been surprised by an oncoming train. At that point they have to decide to die by jumping off the bridge into the water or to die by getting hit by the train. Most have chosen to jump.

Once a young man was on the tracks and had to face this very same decision. He jumped from the bridge and was never found. His girlfriend went back to the tracks for years after the event, hoping to find her boyfriend.

ghost story

The bridge itself is haunted by a woman in white. Often at night, people near the bridge encounter what appears to be a young woman in a white dress walking up and down the train tracks. She has been spotted as far east as the Arcola Trail overpass and as far west as the span crossing the St. Croix River. When she is seen, she never seems to notice the onlookers. She simply walks further down the tracks and sometimes disappears into the night. Many say this woman in white is the girlfriend of the man who fell into the river, and that she is still looking for her lost love.

Sometimes the ghost is carrying a blue lantern in her search for her lost love. Witnesses either see the woman in white or a blue light traveling up and down the tracks at night. The apparitions always eventually dim and fade into the night.

visiting

Arcola Trail North is open to traffic throughout the night. As long as you are not obstructing traffic, you can stop your car under the bridge and watch for hours for the ghost of the mysterious woman in white. The road is rather remote, so it can get very dark and very quiet. This all adds to the creepiness of the place and many times will make this a fun spot to spend a night ghost hunting.

More recently, this has become a popular spot for teenagers to go to get scared and to fool around. As a result of this, police patrol this road rather frequently. If your car is stopped near the bridge and the police catch you there, they will ask you to leave. If you have stepped out of your car and attempted to walk out onto the bridge, you will be arrested.

BLUFF PARK

Concord Street and Highway 52 Ramp, St. Paul,
Minnesota 55107

directions

Take US-52 from downtown St. Paul across the Mississippi River at the Lafayette
Bridge. Follow US-52 for about a mile and a half after the bridge until you get to the
Concord Street exit. At the end of the exit ramp, turn right onto Cesar Chavez Street.
Immediately on your left you will see the entrance to Bluff Park.

history

While at first glance this may appear to be a simple, wooded park in the suburbs of St.
Paul, a piece of history about this place changes the park's entire atmosphere.

The dark history of Bluff Park involves a man who entered the park late one
night with a single goal. He was coming to the dark woods of the park to kill himself.
He made his way deep into a secluded section of the woods and got out the gun with
which he planned to commit the terrible deed. As he stood there in the dark, there was
still a part of him that wanted to live. In a last-ditch effort to either cry for help or to

psyche himself up enough to commit suicide, he yelled out into the night as loud as he could that he was going to kill himself. Campers who were spending the night in the park heard his cry for help.

Then they heard a gunshot.

ghost story

The ghost at Bluff Park seems to be an eerie replay of that terrible night when the man killed himself. No one really ever reports seeing any apparitions or experiencing anything but an auditory reenactment of that night's event. The phenomenon is reported most often by people who are camping for the night. The ghostly sounds are always heard at night.

People hear a man screaming through the woods, "I'm going to kill myself." Often, this exclamation is followed by a gunshot. Those who hear the cry for help and the gunshot often search through the woods for the man. They never find him. Sometimes they even report the incident to the authorities, who never find anything when they search the park for a suicide victim.

visiting

The wooded park is open throughout the night, and people sometimes camp here. There has never been a report of this phenomenon by anyone who was visiting the park during the day, so if you want to find this ghost, you will have to go there at night. If you want a better chance of experiencing this ghost, set up camp and spend the night in the haunted park.

BRAEMAR GOLF COURSE

6364 John Harris Drive, Edina, Minnesota 55439

directions

Take I-394 West from downtown Minneapolis for a little more than 3 miles to exit 5, MN-100 South. Follow MN-100 South for almost 7 miles to the Industrial Boulevard exit. Turn right onto Edina Industrial Boulevard and then take the third right onto West 78th Street. After a little more than half a mile, turn right onto Gleason Road and then after another half mile turn left onto Braemar Boulevard. Take a left onto John Harris Drive and the entrance to the golf course will be on your right.

history

Before this area was a golf course, it was heavily wooded and overgrown. When the developers purchased the land, they needed to clear the area out to create the course. As they were clearing the land, they discovered a homeless African American man who had been living in the woods. He was not in good shape, and the only information they could glean from him was that his name was Jim.

Due to his apparently poor health, they immediately sent him to a hospital, but it was too late. The man died shortly after arriving at the hospital.

ghost story

The golf course is haunted by the ghost of the homeless man who was discovered here. Apparently, he doesn't like golfers much. Every once in a while, someone on the course will see an African American man who walks across a fairway before mysteriously vanishing. These sightings are few and far between though, and most of the paranormal activity has to do with the actual playing of the game.

Apparently, Jim doesn't like golfers getting the ball in the hole. Sometimes, people will place a nice shot that goes right in the hole, and then the ball will simply jump back out of the hole by itself. Other times, people will putt the ball in a straight line towards the hole, and it will seem sure to go in. Suddenly though, the ball will veer off to the right or left as if someone had walked up to the ball and kicked it away.

visiting

In order to experience the ghostly happenings on this golf course, you will have to play a round of golf, so contact the course and reserve a tee time. For a full round of golf, it costs $37, and for 9 holes of golf, it costs $19. It's a beautiful course that is well worth the money—and if you play a bad game, you can always just blame Jim.

CARLOS AVERY STATE WILDLIFE MANAGEMENT AREA

6235 West Broadway Avenue, Forest Lake, Minnesota 55025

directions

From downtown Minneapolis, take I-35W North for about 14.5 miles to exit 33, the Lexington Avenue exit. Turn left onto Lexington Avenue and follow it for about 9.5 miles. Turn right onto West Broadway Avenue. A main entrance to the wildlife management area will be on your left beyond the wrought iron gates. The haunted area actually includes a large area that is in and around the wildlife management preserve. This includes roads in the area such as Old Gamefarm Road, Headquarters Road, Zodiac Street, and other nearby roads.

history

The history of this wildlife management area can be traced back to 1933, when Crex Carpet used the core 8,000 acres of the current wildlife management area as farmland for wire grass used in much of their carpeting. Preservationist and state game and fish commissioner Carlos Avery purchased the land in 1933 to help preserve the Bob White quail, a bird that was endangered in the area.

In 1935, the WPA provided enough money for several buildings and other facilities to be built on the grounds. The wildlife management area and the eleven buildings that make up the facilities were eventually placed on the National Register for Historic Places. Today it is used as a hunting area to help control animal populations, and it's also used as a wildlife sanctuary. Some suggest this place is a sanctuary for something else.

ghost story

For some reason, ghost cars seem to haunt this area. People driving through the area in and around the Carlos Avery State Wildlife Management Area at dusk or at night often notice headlights. Sometimes these headlights mysteriously disappear without there having been any place that the car could have turned off. More frequently, these headlights will be in impossible places. Witnesses will spot headlights to their right and will be shocked when they realize that the area where the headlights appeared is a pool or swamp.

These ghost cars aren't the most famous mystery to haunt these woods. This area is home to the cryptozoological creature called the Linwood Wooly Beast. As early as the 1970s, people in the area have reported seeing a strange creature with the head of a goat on the body of a moose. The creature is typically described as being completely white and somewhat aggressive. While people have seen it crossing the road in front of them or running through a nearby field, they have also reported the creature charging at oncoming vehicles or approaching stopped vehicles to investigate them.

visiting

Many of the roads that traverse the remote sections of the wildlife preserve are unpaved and can get waterlogged and muddy. There is a danger of getting stuck, especially if you enter the preserve after a significant rain or snow and the road is unpaved. Also, pay close attention to any postings that describe visiting hours to the park. Many of the surrounding roads are open throughout the night, and the beast is typically only seen after dark, but there are some sections of the park that do have posted hours.

If you come across the Linwood Wooly Beast, you might want to stay in your car. Even though, reportedly, it has never hurt anyone, it is aggressive—so be cautious.

DEAD MAN'S HILL

14113 Galaxie Avenue, Apple Valley, Minnesota 56208

directions

Take I-35E South from St. Paul for a little more than 14 miles to exit 92, the Cedar Avenue exit. Take the exit to the south towards the zoo and follow Cedar Avenue for another 3 miles. Turn left onto 140th Street West and follow that for half a mile until you get to Galaxie Avenue, which is your first right. There is an entrance to Scott Park on your right. Dead Man's Hill is inside Scott Park.

history

For a while, other than bumps and bruises, there were really no injuries to speak of at the hill. This all changed in 1998 when something tragic happened to a young boy on the hill.

The story goes that a young boy, Dameon, was sledding down the back hill at Dead Man's Hill when he was killed. Apparently, an archer at the adjacent archery range shot an arrow that strayed from its target and struck Dameon in the eye. Mortally wounded, Dameon writhed in pain until finally striking a tree and dying.

ghost story

It seems that Dameon is still sledding down the hill after all these years. Most of the time, the ghostly happenings occur here at night. People do a lot of night sledding on the back hill of Dead Man's Hill, and from time to time, these sledders report encounters with the ghost of Dameon.

Most of the time, people hear moaning, as if someone were in pain. When they investigate the sounds, they are unable to find any source for the moaning. Sometimes, people actually see the apparition of Dameon sledding down the hill and then suddenly disappearing. The apparition is seen exclusively by children—adults never report seeing the ghost.

Sometimes, the ghost becomes a little more dangerous. People sledding down the hill have reported that an unseen force, perhaps the ghost of Dameon, suddenly pushes them so that they run into trees or other obstacles along the slope.

visiting

The ghost is seen and experienced most often by people sledding down the back slope of Dead Man's Hill—and experienced exclusively at night. Only children can see the apparition, but adults can experience other facets of the haunting, such as the moaning or getting pushed into obstacles. In order to experience this ghost, you may need to actually sled down the slope after dark. The park is open until 10 p.m., so that should be doable—and legal. Just be careful: remember that the ghost likes to push unsuspecting sledders into trees.

DEAD MAN'S POND

8227 Ideal Avenue South, Cottage Grove, Minnesota 55016

directions

From downtown St. Paul, take Shepard Road East for about 2.5 miles until it dead-ends into US-10. Take US-10 South for about 9 miles until you reach the 80th Street exit. At the end of the exit, turn left onto 80th Street and follow it for a little more than a mile. Turn right onto Hyde Avenue South and then take the second left onto Ideal Avenue South. Ideal Park will be on your right. Dead Man's Pond, shaped like a teardrop, is the only pond within the park. During some of the year, it is not a pond at all but just a muddy depression in the ground.

history

The ghost stories involve a small boy who decided to go swimming in the pond one day. The boy was an able swimmer and was having fun splashing about by himself until he neared the center of the pond. As the boy swam over the center of the pond, something seemed to grab him from underneath the water and violently pull him under. By the time anyone could get to the middle of the pond to save him, it was too late. The boy had already drowned. No one was able to find what may have pulled him under the water so violently.

ghost story

There are only two ghost stories here at the pond, and they are both rather strange. The first story that circulates is that every once in a while bubbles emerge from the middle of the pond. There is no reason that bubbles should appear there. According to legend, these bubbles are a replay of the last exhalation of the boy who drowned here.

The other story about the pond involves the wildlife that often inhabits the pond. Apparently, the ducks that frequent the pond will not approach its center. The ducks often hang around on the edges of the pond, but even when swimming from one side to the other, they avoid the middle of the pond at all costs. Perhaps there is something there, waiting for its next victim.

visiting

The pond is small and looks almost like a teardrop in the middle of the park. It is possible that the pond could be completely empty since it is so small that the water evaporates during some parts of the summer. It doesn't seem to matter what time of the day you visit the park, because the phenomena with the ducks and the bubbles seem to happen almost constantly. It is definitely creepier, though, to visit the haunted pond after dark, which is possible since the park does not close until 10:30 each night. During most of the year, this is long after dark. Of course, if you visit in winter and the pond is frozen, you will not be able to experience any of the strange occurrences at the pond.

FORT SNELLING

Historic Fort Road, St. Paul, Minnesota 55111

directions

From downtown St. Paul, take I-35E South for about 3.5 miles until you reach exit 103B, the MN-5/West 7th Street exit. At the end of the exit ramp, turn right onto Fort Road and follow that for another 2.5 miles. Take the MN-55 West ramp and then take the ramp towards Fort Snelling. Stay straight to go onto Tower Road and then turn right onto Historic Fort Road. This road will take you onto the grounds and to the historic fort.

history

Construction began on this fort in 1820. It was constructed on a bluff overlooking both the Mississippi and Missouri Rivers and was used to control American interests in the area. Those stationed at the fort were there to make sure that the Native Americans did not attack European settlers and that the European settlers did not settle land that was not sanctioned by the federal government. Eventually, with the rapid growth of Minneapolis and St. Paul, the fort became unnecessary.

When the Civil War broke out, the fort was once again used to train soldiers and to defend the cities of Minneapolis and St. Paul. In 1862, an uprising of the Dakota tribe of Native Americans resulted in the Dakota War of 1862. A group of Dakota out on a hunting expedition came across and killed five European settlers because they blamed all whites for the treaty violations that had brought hard times upon the tribe. Fearing retaliation from Fort Snelling, the Dakota decided to kill as many settlers as they could in an attempt to drive them from the area permanently. They killed as many as 800 settlers before the uprising was quelled. They enslaved and tortured many more settlers before the war was over. Sixteen hundred Dakota were captured and imprisoned in a concentration camp on the grounds of Fort Snelling. Many died while imprisoned there; 303 more Dakota were sentenced to death. President Abraham Lincoln, upon reviewing the trials for the condemned men, decided that all but 39 of the men acted as if at war with the United States and therefore had not committed capital crimes. Thirty-eight of the 39 men were hung in the largest mass execution in American history.

The fort was used again during WW II but soon afterwards fell into disrepair. In 1960, the fort was listed on the National Register for Historic Places and was restored by the Minnesota Historical Society, which still runs the fort to this day.

ghost story

Both the park below the fort and the fort itself are reputed to be haunted. In the park below the fort where the concentration camp was located, people report being touched by unseen forces and hearing people talking in a language they do not understand. From the park, people also report strange things when looking up at the fort itself—figures dressed in 19th-century military uniforms in the windows and strange lights going up and down the stairs of the towers.

Inside of the building, people again get touched by invisible forces and experience intangible feelings of discomfort. They will feel as if they are being watched or as if there is something there that does not want them there. Others see figures walking through the corridors that mysteriously vanish without a trace.

visiting

From Memorial Day until Labor Day, the fort is open to the public every day of the week, except Monday, until 5 p.m. From Labor Day until Halloween, the fort is only open on Saturdays and only until 5 p.m. Admission is $10. This is your only chance to investigate the fort itself and experience the paranormal happenings within the fortified walls.

The park that surrounds the historic fort is open throughout the year and every day of the week. The park is only open until 4 p.m., though, so you would have to go before 4 p.m. if you are interested in looking up at the fort and perhaps seeing the apparition of a soldier looking back down at you.

FOUNTAIN LAKE

370 72nd Street SE, Montrose, Minnesota 55363

directions

From Minneapolis, take I-394 West and follow it for a little more than 9 miles until you come to the US-12 West exit on your left. Follow US-12 West for a little more than 24 miles until you get to Meridian Avenue South. Turn left onto Meridian Avenue and then take the first left onto 72nd Street SE. In less than half a mile, you will see the large Fountain Lake on your right. Roads surround most of the lake, but most places near the lakeshore are residential properties.

history

Montrose and Delano are both towns that lay some claim to the shore of the massive lake. Originally, the area was inhabited by an early native mound-building culture that often built burial mounds along lakeshores. After these early natives, the area was inhabited by the Dakota tribe (also known as Sioux). In the mid-1800s, a tribe of Native Americans known as the Chippewa moved west from Lake Superior to this area, and war commenced between the two tribes. Eventually, the Native Americans were pushed out of the area, and the European settlers would eventually use Fountain Lake as a fishing and recreational lake.

One inhabitant of Delano met with tragedy in the lake. A young woman was on a boat when somehow she was tossed into the lake. The lake was by no means calm at the time, and no matter how much she struggled, she was eventually pulled under the waves. Others in the area were able to hear her screams, but they were unable to get to her in time. Her body was never found.

ghost story

The ghost of the young woman who was killed in the lake still haunts these waters to this day. People who have experienced her ghost have either been on the lake or on the shore late at night. These witnesses hear frantic splashing and a woman screaming, begging anyone who can hear her to help her. No matter how hard these would-be rescuers search, they are never able to find any sign of a woman in the water.

visiting

Most of the time this ghost is experienced at midnight or very close to midnight. This would undoubtedly make midnight the best time to go out looking for this ghost. If you don't have a boat or access to the lake itself, your best vantage point for finding this ghost is on the north shore of the lake. It is possible to park your car along the road on the shore here and look out across the haunted lake. The north shore and the south shore on 82nd Street SE are the only parts of the lakeshore that are not occupied by residential houses.

GREY CLOUD ISLAND
Grey Cloud Island, Minnesota 55071

directions

Take Warner Road from downtown St. Paul to US-10 East and follow US-10 for 7 miles. Take the County Road 22 exit and turn right onto Summit Avenue. Take the first right onto St. Paul Park Road and then the first left onto 3rd Street. Follow 3rd Street for about 2.5 miles. It will change its name to Grey Cloud Island Drive South and take you across a bridge onto the island. The entire island is reputed to be haunted.

history

There is a higher concentration of Native American burial mounds on this island than anywhere else. It was inhabited by the Woodland Mound Builder culture as early as 100 B.C.E. and had been an area of settlement for Native Americans until 1838. In 1838, a treaty between the Dakota and the European settlers forced the last Native American settlers on the island to move west of the Mississippi River.

Europeans soon moved into the structures that still stood on the island. The first settlers were two fur traders, the younger of which had married a Native American woman. He named the island after his wife's mother, whose name was Grey Cloud.

Throughout the years since 1838, the island has remained sparsely populated. For a while there was a lime kiln on the island that was used to make mortar. The kiln still stands today but has not been used for many decades. Today, the area is a National River and Recreation Area with the National Park Service. There are still some people living on the island, but the population density is much less than that of the surrounding areas—perhaps because some people are scared of the island after dark.

ghost story

After the sun sets on Grey Cloud Island, the ghosts come out. The ghostly occurrences on the island are all visual. People actually see these ghosts, and despite the denials of the residents, they tend to see them often.

Perhaps the most-often-seen ghosts on the island are strange lights. People encounter strange balls of light floating around on all parts of the island. People driving the streets see them floating nearby in a field or actually crossing the street in front of them. The balls of light are most often seen in the wooded areas of the island.

People also run across an apparition of a Native American man in full Dakota dress, perhaps Chief Medicine Bottle himself, the last Native American leader to inhabit the island. Again, this apparition is encountered throughout the island but only after darkness falls.

Finally, people see a motorcyclist riding the roads of Grey Cloud Island at night. Alarmingly, the rider and bike are both translucent, and they make no sound as they roll along.

visiting

There are things that make finding these ghosts easy and things that make finding them difficult. On the easy side, the roads of Grey Cloud Island are all public roads and are open throughout the night. You are able to go late at night when there are no other drivers on the road and traverse the haunted island for as long as you need in hopes of sighting one of the apparitions.

Unfortunately, there are things that you need to look out for and pay attention to when visiting the island, especially at night. Many of the island residents absolutely deny that there are any ghosts here, and they hate ghost explorers who come onto their island looking for ghosts—mainly because of vandalism reportedly caused by ghost hunters. If you are on the island at night, do not step upon any ground that may be private property. Pay attention to all applicable laws and make sure that you do not do anything to disturb the island's residents.

HOLBROOK PARK

310 Harrington Drive, Long Lake, Minnesota 55356

directions

From downtown Minneapolis, take I-394 West for about 9.5 miles to the end of the Interstate. Exit to the left onto US-12 and follow US-12 for an additional 4.5 miles. Exit US-12 onto Wayzata Boulevard West and follow this road for a little more than 2 miles. Turn left onto Brown Road and then take the second right onto Grand Avenue. Turn right onto Harrington Drive after less than half a mile, and the park will be on your right.

history

Long Lake, Minnesota, was first settled by Europeans in the mid-1800s. In its early years, it was much like many other early settlements of the time. The Native Americans who called the area home were moved away, and houses, stores, and mills popped up throughout the area. The town continued to grow, and by the 1890s residents realized they were in the perfect climate to grow many different types of berries.

The town began to boom in population at that time, as it became a center for berry production. Berries from Long Lake were shipped to many parts of the country, and to this day, the town owes its size and history to the berries that were grown here.

ghost story

Many things about the ghosts at Holbrook Park are very specific and are repeated almost exactly every time the ghosts are seen. First, the ghosts are only seen on Sunday night. There has never been a report of the ghosts here spotted on any day of the week other than Sunday. Next, the ghosts appear at a very specific time—only between midnight and 2 a.m.

Two ghosts are seen here. The first ghost is that of a little girl, who always looks lost and frightened when she is by herself. Many witnesses approach her with the intention of trying to help her, but will soon regret that decision when she mysteriously vanishes.

Other times, the little girl ghost is seen with her father. When she is with her father, she does not seem frightened but is instead happily gathering berries into her apron. If you approach the girl when her father is there, the girl will disappear but the father will attack. People who approach them at night have scratch marks on their body that have no source, and they sometimes feel as if something had just punched them in the stomach.

visiting

While it usually makes it easier to find the ghosts in an area when you know the exact time that they come out; in this case, it makes it a little bit harder. Holbrook Park closes at 10 p.m. This is long after dark many nights of the year, but the ghosts don't come out until sometime between midnight and 2 a.m. This doesn't make it impossible for us law-abiding paranormal explorers to find the ghosts though. Luckily, there are many public roads that run alongside the park. As long as you do not enter the park grounds, you can drive or walk around the edge of the park looking in to see the ghosts. Be sure that you keep your eye on your watch though; it is illegal to park on any street in Long Lake after 2 a.m.

INDIAN MOUNDS PARK

10 Mounds Boulevard, St. Paul, Minnesota 55106

directions

From downtown St. Paul, take Kellogg Avenue East for a mile until you get to Mounds Boulevard. Follow Mounds Boulevard for about a mile, and it will take you directly into the park. The park will be both on your left and your right.

history

Today, only six Native American burial mounds remain in this park overlooking the skyline of St. Paul. It is thought that within the last 2,000 years, at least 16 mounds were once present in the area. Some of the mounds were simply destroyed by weather and people over the years. Others were excavated in the 19th century. Preservation was not a top priority for excavations during this time period. Today, the six remaining mounds are protected.

The first of the mounds in this area was thought to have been built by the Hopewell culture nearly 2,000 years ago. Later Native American cultures likely destroyed some of the original mounds and built some of their own. Perhaps more than 2,000 years of Native American burials have taken place in this area.

ghost story

Perhaps the most frequently reported paranormal phenomenon in the park is people hearing footsteps walking through the grass near the burial mounds. No matter how hard the witnesses search, no source is ever found for these footsteps.

People also experience intangible feelings of discomfort. Some feel like they are being watched even when there is no one nearby. Others simply feel unwelcome and want to leave. People have also smelled meat cooking and have heard children crying while within this park.

visiting

The park is open until 11 p.m. every day of the week and every week of the year. The best time to enter the park to look for ghosts is after dark. The best places to search are remote areas where not many people are around whom you may mistake for a paranormal entity.

LAKE REBECCA PARK RESERVE

9831 Rebecca Park Trail, Rockford, Minnesota 55373

directions

From downtown Minneapolis, take I-394 West for a little more than 9 miles until you get to the US-12 exit on the left of the highway. Follow US-12 West for 17 miles and then turn right onto County Line Road Southeast. Follow this for about 2.5 miles and this takes you into the park itself.

history

Lake Rebecca Park is a beautiful park that surrounds several small lakes, the largest of which is called Lake Rebecca. The park offers hiking trails, boating opportunities, and play areas for children.

The darker history of this area involves a man who was depressed and walking one of the trails with the intent of ending his own life. He found a particularly remote section of a trail with a remarkable view of Lake Rebecca and sat on a bench to further contemplate suicide. Deciding to go through with it, he pulled out a gun and shot himself in the head. His body was not found until the next day.

ghost story

The bench where the man shot himself is supposedly haunted. When people are walking or jogging the trail alone, especially in the evening, they see a man sitting on a bench overlooking the lake. These witnesses don't think much of it until they get closer and realize the man has a gaping bullet wound in his head. Soon after the witnesses notice this wound in his head, he vanishes. He often watches people as they approach on the trail, his eyes vacant and creepy.

While this ghost is most often seen sitting on the bench, he has also been spotted slowly walking along the trails in the area where he killed himself. He again vacantly stares at approaching hikers, who notice the bullet hole in his head before he vanishes.

visiting

This park opens at 5 a.m. and is open until 10 p.m. These are the only times you can walk the trails looking for the ghost of the man who shot himself. This is okay because it gets dark before 10 p.m., and you are able to walk the trails at night. Just make sure you bring sufficient light and that you leave yourself enough time to exit the park before it closes.

The trails the man is seen at most often are the two that cross near the southwestern corner of Lake Rebecca. There is a paved trail and an unpaved trail near the southwestern lakeshore. The ghost is seen most often on benches in this area.

LEBANON HILLS REGIONAL PARK

860 Cliff Road, Eagan, Minnesota 55123

directions

Take I-35E South from downtown St. Paul for about 10 miles to exit 97A, Pilot Knob Road. Follow Pilot Knob Road for a little more than 3 miles to Cliff Road. Turn left onto Cliff Road and follow it for about 2 miles. The park visitor center will be on your right. The ghosts here are at the many lakes and trails that are interspersed throughout the park.

history

Dakota County was home to a tribe of Dakota Native Americans during the late 1700s when French explorers were first setting foot in the area. By 1819, European settlers had created a fort in the area, and relations between the settlers and the Native Americans were getting tense. By 1851, the European presence in the area was so overwhelming that the Dakota were forced to sell off their land or face military action from the stronger European force. In 1851, all of the sacred land in what is today Dakota County was abandoned by the native people and taken over by European settlers.

While Lebanon Hills Park itself is relatively new, the beautiful landscape and lakes have been around and have been explored and visited by people as long as the people have been around. There are stories from the older days, decades ago, about people, especially children, who have gone to visit the area and then simply never returned.

ghost story

It is hard to explain exactly what reportedly goes on in Lebanon Hills Park after dark. The best way to explain it is to start with perhaps the strangest of paranormal reports. Several lakes are situated in and around Lebanon Hills Regional Park. At night, from time to time, people witness a bright swirling glow that comes from the middle of a lake. Some describe it as a kind of portal. Others describe it as a large glowing platform in the middle of the lake. Some have seen a woman standing in the middle of this strange glow, beckoning to onlookers to join her in the center of the lake. The ones who tell these stories never go out to the middle of the lake. Perhaps there are others who do.

The trails and woods throughout the area are haunted. People sometimes hear a female voice coming from the woods. Sometimes, the woman's voice sounds frightened and panicked. Sometimes, those who hear her can make out the words "Help me." Sometimes these words are followed by screaming. The helpless witnesses search for the woman but never find any sign of her no matter how long they look.

Perhaps the most often encountered ghosts in the park are the sounds of laughter coming from small children. People walking the trails alone in remote sections of the park hear children laughing from the forest. Often they search for the children but find no sign of them anywhere.

visiting

The park itself is open throughout the night and allows camping along with many other activities. The portals and ghostly sounds seem to occur all over the park. There is not a specific lake where the portal is seen, and there is not a specific trail where the woman and children are heard. The only thing that seems to be uniform with the descriptions, besides the ghosts themselves, is that the people who experience them seem to be alone or with small groups of people. There are places within the park where you can be quite isolated from anyone else—these are areas where the ghosts come out to play.

LILYDALE PARK
950 Lilydale Road, Lilydale, Minnesota 55118

directions

From St. Paul, take Wabasha Street to the south over the Mississippi River. Follow this road for about a half mile until you reach Plato Boulevard. Turn right onto Plato Boulevard West. Follow Plato for a half mile until you get to the Harbor Road Raise. Turn left onto Harbor Road Raise. Harbor Road becomes Water Street West. Follow Water Street for about a mile and a half until it changes its name to Lilydale Road. The park will be on your left.

history

Lilydale Park is an undeveloped park just outside of St. Paul, Minnesota. From the Mississippi River bluffs, you can see a spectacular view of the city skyline. The place is riddled with prehistoric geological and biological artifacts. Fossils are easy to find and caves dot the landscape.

For a while, the area was used as a brick-making factory. The owners of the factory chose the site because of all of the readily available clay. Today the factory is gone, but there are still remnants in the form of bricks and parts of buildings. Many of the caves in the area were made during the life of the brick factory and have been abandoned since the early 1900s. They are currently closed to the public.

Since the area has never been a developed park and many of the areas in the park are somewhat remote, the area at one time gained a rather dark reputation. Many people have committed suicide within the park, either throwing themselves from the bluffs or killing themselves in other ways on some of the remote trails. Several reported murders and rapes have occurred within the park as well.

ghost story

Several spirits haunt this park, and they appear at any time of the day—most often when the witnesses are alone in the park.

The ghosts heard most often here are children. Witnesses hear what sound like screaming children coming from all around them. These screams are heard most often near the caves. Whenever those hearing the screams try to find their source, no children are ever found.

People also encounter white, misty apparitions throughout the entire park. These apparitions float through the woods and the trails and then mysteriously disappear. Perhaps these are remnants of those people who met their untimely end here in the park.

visiting

The ghosts are said to haunt the areas outside of the caves, so the fact that the caves are closed for the public's safety has no impact on your search for the ghosts here. The ghosts are not exclusively seen at night, so you have an opportunity to go to the park at any time in order to hunt for the apparitions and listen for the children here. The ghosts manifest most often when the witness is alone or in a small group. If you are walking through the park alone, be careful though. There are some dangerous trails and the area is rather remote. In addition, there have been documented rapes and murders within the park. If you go, be careful. You may want to stay away from the place at night.

MINNESOTA STATE FAIRGROUNDS

1265 North Snelling Avenue N., St. Paul, Minnesota

directions

From St. Paul, take I-94 North for about 3 miles to exit 238, Snelling Avenue. At the end of the exit ramp, turn right onto Snelling Avenue. Follow Snelling Avenue for a little more than 2 miles. The Minnesota State Fairgrounds will be on your left. They are huge and you can't miss them. To get to the grandstand, take a left onto Dan Patch Avenue.

history

The first state fair to occur on these fairgrounds started on September 7, 1885. The site was chosen because it was about halfway between Minneapolis and St. Paul. Each city had previously had its own fair, and the state wanted to hold just one giant fair everyone could attend. As the years have passed and attendance has increased, the Minnesota State Fair has become the largest fair in the United States in terms of daily attendance.

On September 7, 1901, a week to the day before becoming President of the United States, Theodore Roosevelt made an appearance at the Minnesota State Fair.

During this appearance, he made the most famous statement of his career, "Speak softly and carry a big stick."

Many of the buildings and rides in the fairgrounds have been around for many years. The oldest ride in the fairgrounds, Ye Old Mill, was built in 1915. It is a series of dark tunnels that you float through on a small boat. Children's music plays in the background, and small fairy tale scenes are displayed from time to time throughout the ride.

ghost story

A couple ghosts supposedly haunt the fairgrounds. The first ghost is that of a young blond man who is always spotted in the grandstand area. While many times this young man is seen at night, he is also occasionally seen in broad daylight. Witnesses who encounter this apparition see him walking around before he mysteriously vanishes into thin air. He is seen most often near a small building behind the grandstand stage that the employees refer to as "The Bunker."

The other ghost haunts the area around Ye Old Mill ride at the fairgrounds just off Wright Avenue, adjacent to the grandstand. For many years, a man named Wayne Murray was a maintenance worker at Ye Old Mill ride. Murray passed away in 1986, and soon after his death, something strange began to happen at the fairgrounds. Every year since 1986, a small brown bird flies into the fairgrounds and disappears into Ye Old Mill ride. Those who have witnessed this bird appear year after year for the fair say that it is perhaps the ghost of Wayne Murray, keeping an eye on the ride that he spent so much time working on.

Other witnesses report strange things happening while riding Ye Old Mill ride. People will feel a presence behind them in the boat even though there is no one there. Others feel someone tap them on their shoulder despite there being no one behind them.

visiting

The fairgrounds are open for the Minnesota State Fair for 12 days a year. The fair ends on Labor Day, so it typically runs from the end of August until Labor Day in September. This is the only time that you are able to actually ride Ye Old Mill ride. The fairgrounds are open from time to time throughout the rest of the year, though, as other events are regularly held at the fairgrounds. These other events are constantly changing, so you need to check the schedule of events on their Web site in order to tell when the grounds are open to the public.

MONTGOMERY NATIONAL GOLF CLUB

900 Rogers Drive, Montgomery, Minnesota 56069

directions

From downtown Minneapolis, take I-35W South for about 16.5 miles. I-35W South will change to I-35 South. Continue to follow the highway for another 21 miles until you get to exit 66, the Montgomery exit. At the end of the exit ramp, turn right onto Millersburg Boulevard West and follow this road for another 7.5 miles. Turn right onto Independence Avenue and then take the first left onto 100th Street West. Follow 100th for a little more than 6 miles and then turn right onto Deer Trail South. After another half mile, turn left onto Deer Trail and then right onto Rogers Drive. This will take you directly into the golf course.

history

While this site has been a golf course since the early 1970s, the land itself once was comprised of farmland. The farmland was owned by a man named Alfred Bury, and for many years, he and his family lived and worked on this land on the outskirts of Montgomery. Alfred Bury died in the 1960s, and eventually his wife sold the farmland, which was turned into the golf course. At least four of the early settlers who worked this farmland in the mid-1800s are buried on the property. Their headstones are still standing. They are currently positioned near the first hole of the golf course.

The course itself was designed in the early 1970s by a famous golf course designer named Joel Goldstrand. The course was originally only nine holes, but was eventually expanded to 18 holes in 1994. Since that time, it has become one of the most popular and beautiful golf courses in the area.

ghost story

The ghosts here at the Montgomery National Golf Club are typically spotted as the golf course is closing for the night. Employees who are closing down the clubhouse often see these ghosts from inside the building. The first ghost is reputed to be one of the early farmers of the property who is buried near Hole #1. People see a man on the golf course in overalls and a straw hat. From time to time, employees approach the man to inform him that the course has closed for the evening, but as they approach, the man mysteriously vanishes.

The other ghost at the course is reputed to be one of the early owners of the golf course who had since passed away. This ghost is typically seen inside of the clubhouse. Near closing time, employees see him sitting at the bar for a split second before he disappears. Other times, people see him standing outside a window of the clubhouse. He vanishes shortly after being spotted.

Besides these two apparitions, other strange things happen within the clubhouse. Televisions turn on and off by themselves, and the thermostat drops to almost freezing temperatures for no reason.

visiting

It's rather difficult for someone who doesn't golf to experience the ghosts here at the course. If you are a golfer, you can always reserve one of the later tee times so that you are finishing your game around the time the course closes. If you have a tee time, you can hang out in the clubhouse and perhaps experience some ghostly activity there.

For those of us who are not golfers, it is a little harder to find these ghosts. If you are not there to golf, you shouldn't enter the property. Since the apparition of the farmer is often seen throughout the course near closing time, however, there are places you can go and perhaps spot him still. Northside Park on Rogers Drive touches the course, and you can go there and look for a ghost on the course. There are also public roads surrounding the course from which you can watch the course for a man with overalls and a straw hat.

SELTZ' POINT AT LAKE COMO

1360 Lexington Parkway North, St. Paul, Minnesota 55103

directions

Take I-94 West from downtown St. Paul for about 2 miles until you reach exit 239B, the Lexington Parkway exit. Turn right onto Lexington Parkway North and follow it for another 2 miles. This will take you into Lake Como Park and to the shores of Lake Como.

history

The ghostly history of this beautiful lake in the middle of Como Park can be traced all the way to Northfield, Minnesota, and all the way back to September 7, 1876. This was the location and date of perhaps the most famous bank robbery in the history of Minnesota. One of the most famous outlaw gangs of the time period, the James-Younger Gang, decided to meet outside of Northfield and rob the First National Bank of Northfield because of ties that it shared with Union leadership during the Civil War. At around 2 p.m., three men entered the bank while the other five terrorized the street by firing their weapons into the air. The town would have none of it. From the cover of the surrounding stores, the townspeople opened fire on the robbers. Several were killed, more were wounded, and some escaped.

A posse eventually caught up with the robber Charlie Pitts and killed him in a shootout. The body of Charlie was purchased by a local physician named Henry Hoyt, who wanted to use the body for medical research and display. Before he was able to do anything with the body, Dr. Hoyt was granted an opportunity to travel to Chicago for a few months. Unwilling to let the body go to waste, he placed the body in a coffin and submerged it in the waters of Lake Como at Seltz' Point to preserve it. During the time of Dr. Hoyt's absence, someone discovered the submerged body in the water. The police were called and a murder investigation ensued. Eventually, Hoyt was called back to St. Paul to straighten everything out with the investigation, and throughout the following years, the bones of Charlie Pitts have traveled from museum to medical school throughout the region.

No one is quite sure where the body is today.

ghost story

Rumor has it that the ghost of Charlie Pitts haunts the corner of the lake where his body had been stored. These rumors and legends designate this corner as Seltz' Point. People around this area will sometimes see a man who looks very much like Charlie Pitts walking through the area in the shallows of the lake or along the lakeshore. This man will always seem lost and confused. When he sees someone approaching him, he immediately vanishes without a trace. Others will report being touched or feeling unwelcome when nearing the shoreline at Seltz' Point.

visiting

The tricky part of visiting this particular ghost is that no one seems to be quite sure where Seltz' Point is. We spoke to several employees at a pavilion at the lakeshore who had never heard of Seltz' Point and had worked there for years. Luckily, though, Lake Como itself is neither very large nor very deep. You can easily walk around it by using one of the many sidewalks and trails in the area. Typically, the ghost is experienced during times when the sun is not shining brightly. This means that people have experiences at night, at dusk, or even during rainy days.

SHAKOPEE MEMORIAL PARK

1801 County Road 101, Shakopee, Minnesota 55379

directions

From downtown Minneapolis, take I-35W South for about 7.5 miles to I-494 West. Follow I-494 West for about 4.5 miles to exit 10B, the US-169 South exit. Follow US-169 South for 10 miles and then exit at the Marschall Road ramp. Turn right onto Marschall Road and follow it for a mile and a half before turning right onto First Avenue East. The road will change names to CR-101 and Memorial Park will be on your left.

history

The town of Shakopee, Minnesota, was named after a Dakota chief of the same name. The Dakota tribe once inhabited the land of Shakopee but slowly lost land in deals to the white settlers. By the early 1860s, the Dakota had had enough of the way the white settlers were violating treaties and stealing their land. A band of Dakota rebels killed 800 settlers starting the Dakota War of 1862. Settlers in the Shakopee area were killed during the uprising.

While this event in history could have had something to do with the ghosts in Memorial Park, a much more likely historic scenario for the ghosts occurred as many as 1,800 years earlier than that. Nearly 2,000 years ago, the area was inhabited by the Hopewell culture of Native Americans. In the area that is today Memorial Park, they constructed sacred burial mounds in which they buried their culture's elite. The mounds are still present in the park to this day.

ghost story

There is only one ghost story that is frequently reported from this park. All descriptions of these ghosts are similar and are visual apparitions. People see shadowy figures in the park. These sightings involve as few as one and as many as three figures. The figures run across the park and through the trails—and then simply fade away or vanish.

These figures are frequently seen after dark, and when they vanish, they seem to slowly blend with the surrounding blackness. Those who see them wonder for a fleeting second whether they had really seen anything at all.

visiting

The ghosts that roam this cemetery are seen exclusively at night. For this reason, it is important that you enter the park after dark if you want to see the ghosts. The figures are seen throughout the entire park, but are seen more frequently near the Hopewell burial mounds and the trails near them. The park is open past dark but closes at 10 p.m., so make sure you have left the park by that time.

STURGES PARK

Highway 25 and Second Avenue South, Buffalo,
Minnesota 55313

directions

Take I-394 West from downtown Minneapolis for a little more than 9 miles to the
US-12 exit on the left side of the interstate. Follow US-12 West for a little more than
23 miles before turning right onto State Highway 25 Southeast. Follow State Highway
25 for a little more than 6 miles into Buffalo until you reach the intersection of MN-
25 and Second Avenue South. The park will be on your left on the lakeside.

history

While the area was originally inhabited by Native Americans in the early part of the
region's history, European settlers did finally move into the area in the mid-1800s.
During that time, the area's population was quite low. The area was primarily a
vacation destination for the wealthy in Minneapolis and St. Paul, both of which were

less than an hour from Buffalo by train. Much of the land surrounding Buffalo Lake was used by resorts for these tourists from the big city.

The park itself is named after one of the more successful resort owners in the area. When Sturges ran his businesses in Buffalo, most of the people in Buffalo at that time were tourists. His house actually still stands near the southwestern edge of the park by the lakeshore.

Eventually the land on the lakeshore near Sturges's house became a park for the City of Buffalo. They built playgrounds, ball fields, and public restrooms.

ghost story

At the lakeshore, near the old Sturges house, people will still see a strange figure walking alone. The figure wears 1800s clothing and walks along the lakeshore near the house or actually within the house itself. Whenever this figure is investigated, the witnesses are unable to find the person. The figure either disappears into thin air or simply turns a corner, and the witnesses are unable to find him. It has been suggested that this is the ghost of Old Man Sturges, still roaming his property after all these years.

While the ghost of Old Man Sturges is the ghost here that has the most basis in history, there are other strange things that happen at the park that are quite a bit scarier and quite a bit stranger. This ghostly activity happens at the old restroom in the park. It happens most frequently at night or on dark or dreary days. Sometimes, people see balls of light floating in and out of the old restroom at night. No explanation for these balls of light is ever found. Other times, people walk into the restroom and find disconcerting messages written in blood on the bathroom mirrors. Sometimes the messages are short and curt, saying things like "Help me," or "Get out," but other times there are actually names on the mirrors. Once, a man using the restroom exited the stall to find his own name written in blood on the mirror. He hadn't heard anyone leave or enter the restroom.

visiting

A lot of the ghostly happenings at Sturges Park occur after dark. The bad news is that the park is not open throughout the night. The good news is the park is open until 10 p.m. This means that most evenings, you will be able to roam the park after the sun has set. Keep a close eye on the old restroom since this is where most of the creepiest things take place. Feel free to enter the restroom and see if your name mysteriously appears on the mirror in blood.

SWEDE HOLLOW PARK

275 East Seventh Street, St. Paul, Minnesota 55106

directions

Take Seventh Street to the east from the center of St. Paul, and Swede Hollow Park will be on your left just after you pass Payne Avenue.

history

Formerly, Swede Hollow was the worst slum the Twin Cities area has ever seen. Immigrants moving into the area who couldn't afford to live in any of the better areas of the city would often live in this little hollow near the river. The hollow was surrounded by steep hills and bluffs, atop of which the better neighborhoods in the city sat. These "nicer" neighborhoods used Swede Hollow as a dump, throwing their garbage down into the valley below. Remarkably, the residents of Swede Hollow didn't mind. They would often scavenge through this garbage, looking for usable or saleable items to improve their quality of life.

As the 20th century began to unfold and electricity began to flow through every city in America, Swede Hollow became a notable exception. Electricity lit the houses and heated the buildings of all the surrounding neighborhoods, but Swede Hollow remained powerless. Besides the people who constantly died from hunger and curable diseases in the impoverished area, people died during the area's harsh winters because their buildings were not heated.

While most of St. Paul grew and became more technological over the years, Swede Hollow floundered and became an ugly scar on the city's face. In 1956, the city had had enough, but instead of improving the neighborhood, they went the opposite way. They declared the neighborhood a health hazard to the city and forcibly kicked those who lived there out. Then, with a controlled fire, they burned the neighborhood to the ground.

Today, the neighborhood is a part of Swede Hollow Park. The foundations of several buildings are still apparent within the park, but much of the old neighborhood has been completely overgrown by vegetation. Something terrifying seems to remain, though, from the days when it was the city's slum.

ghost story

Since the old neighborhood that was once here has now been completely abandoned, the area is, by definition, a ghost town. But other things happen here to cement this place's title as a ghost town. Perhaps some of the unfortunate residents who once lived in this area and died here still walk through these grounds as if it were never burned and abandoned.

Most often, people encounter figures in the old neighborhood part of the park, especially near the foundations of the old buildings that are still visible. These figures look like normal people but suddenly disappear. Sometimes these figures appear to be wearing clothing from the early 1900s. Other people who venture into the haunted section of the park hear footsteps when there is no one there or encounter foul smells that seem to have no source.

visiting

While Swede Hollow Park does not post any closing hours, it is not a place you would like to go at night. The neighborhood that surrounds the park is not all that great, and it would be an unnecessary risk to wander around this place after dark. On the other hand, during the day this is a nice, accessible, historically rich park. You can go looking for ghosts just as easily here during the day without undertaking any unnecessary risk.

SECTION II

cemeteries, hospitals, and churches

ANOKA-METRO REGIONAL TREATMENT CENTER

3301 Seventh Avenue North, Anoka, Minnesota 55303

directions

From downtown Minneapolis, take I-94 West for about 4.5 miles. Merge onto MN-252 North and follow that for another 4 miles. From there, merge onto MN-610 East and follow that for 3 miles until you reach MN-47 North. Follow MN-47 North for 7.5 miles to the Seventh Avenue exit, and then turn right at the end of the exit ramp onto Seventh Avenue. After about a half mile, the facility will be on your left.

history

In 1900, the First State Asylum for the Insane was built on this site. While today the facility is called the Anoka-Metro Regional Treatment Center, it is essentially still the same hospital. Throughout the hundred plus years that it has been in existence, it has changed names three times, always to something that sounded less "abrasive" to those held there or those who had family members held there.

Throughout the many years the insane asylum has been in operation, it has become much more technological, informed about its patients' conditions, and, above

all, humane. In the early 1900s, insane asylums were notorious for the inhumane treatment they provided their patients. Although the Anoka State Hospital was never singled out for exceptionally terrible treatment of their patients, the mind set towards the insane and the accepted psychological practices and beliefs of the time suggest that treatment was no different in this asylum.

Patients were tied down, beaten, and forced to do things they did not want to do. Sometimes employees who either didn't want to be there or who enjoyed torturing the "chronic incurables" housed here would torment the patients for the sake of tormenting them. It is no wonder that, when an avenue of escape presented itself to the patients, they took it.

A series of tunnels runs underneath all of the buildings at the facility. These were used to transfer patients from one building to another or to transfer bodies away from the buildings without the other patients seeing them. Many times, patients would attempt to escape by sneaking into the dark tunnels at night. Most of the time, these patients would become hopelessly lost within the tunnels. When they were unable to find their way out and after they had decided they were not going back, they took another way out and hung themselves from the heavy metal pipes that ran through the tunnels.

While conditions at the asylum became much better over the years, death did still occur here. In 1920, an epidemic of influenza hit the asylum, killing more than 100 people. Later, the hospital was also used as a tuberculosis sanitarium. Many died of this incurable disease at the site as well.

ghost story

The ghosts here at this site seem to have confined themselves to the underground tunnels and to the on-site cemetery that was once used for those who died while on site.

The tunnels are mostly haunted by strange sounds. People hear footsteps approaching them within the tunnels but are unable to find their source. People hear angry whispers coming from all around them despite there being no one there. Sourceless laughter sometimes echoes down the tunnels. Cold spots suddenly manifest and dissipate without reason, and people see shadowy figures moving in the darkness in front of them.

The cemetery is also haunted by strange sounds. Witnesses hear the sounds of crying coming from the surrounding woods or hear strange whispers or laughter coming from within the cemetery. People also feel uncomfortable while in the cemetery—unwelcome or depressed.

visiting

Unfortunately, the tunnels at the asylum are essentially inaccessible to ghost hunters. The facility is still in operation, and the only people who have access to the tunnels are maintenance workers.

The cemetery, on the other hand, is completely accessible to the public during daylight hours. It does close at dark, so do not attempt to enter the cemetery after nightfall. You will be arrested for trespassing. That is okay, though, since the strange sounds are apparent in the cemetery during daylight hours.

CALVARY CEMETERY

4200 Eagle Creek Boulevard, Shakopee, Minnesota 55379

directions

Take I-35W South from downtown Minneapolis for about 7.5 miles until you reach I-494 West. Follow I-494 for another 5 miles to US-169 South at exit 10B. Follow US-169 for 8 miles to the Canterbury Road exit. Turn left onto Canterbury Road and follow it for a half mile before turning left onto Eagle Creek Boulevard. The cemetery will be on the left.

history

This cemetery was built on the site of one of the first residences in Shakopee, an old farm that dates back to the mid-1800s. Eventually, more and more people moved into the area, making Shakopee a town all its own and in need of a place to bury their dead. This site was designated as the town's first cemetery. Many of the oldest families and original pioneers from the area are buried here.

More recently, suburban construction has all but completely surrounded the cemetery. It is a piece of history being slowly swallowed by modern suburban sprawl. On a small hill behind the cemetery is a subdivision called Howard's Edition. Sometimes the cemetery is called Howard's Edition Cemetery. Is this because of the cemetery's proximity to the subdivision, or is it because something seems to have escaped the cemetery and has wandered into Howard's Edition?

ghost story

Every once in a while, people from the surrounding houses report a break-in. This is odd because, first, this is a good neighborhood. Crimes such as this are almost unheard of in the area. The second reason this is odd is because there is plenty of evidence that someone was there, but nothing is ever taken. Cabinets and cupboards have been opened and their contents strewn about. Muddy footprints have been tracked throughout the house. Nothing is taken. The doors and windows are locked.

The victims of these strange crimes blame the cemetery. They know the cemetery is haunted. They simply clean up and go on with their lives. Cars that drive by the cemetery at night sometimes stall out or completely die directly in front of the cemetery. Others who peer into the cemetery after dark see a little boy in 19th-century clothing lurking in the cemetery. If the boy spots you, he will hide behind a tree and then peer at you from behind the tree until you either approach or walk away.

visiting

The cemetery closes at dark, and the houses that surround it are private residences. Make sure that if you approach the fence that surrounds the cemetery, you are respectful of the people who live close by, who are likely sleeping. From outside the fence, you can look into the cemetery at night for the little boy. You can also drive your car by the cemetery at any time to see if it dies for no reason.

COTTAGE GROVE HISTORICAL CEMETERY

10999 70th Street, Cottage Grove, Minnesota 55016

directions

From downtown St. Paul, take Shepard Road East for about 2.5 miles until it dead-ends into US-10. Take US-10 South for about 4 miles until you reach the Bailey Road exit. At the end of the exit ramp, turn left onto Bailey Road and follow it for about a mile. Turn right onto Military Road and follow it for a little more than 5 miles. Military Road will change its name to 70th Street West. About a mile further down the road, Cottage Grove Historical Cemetery will be on your right.

history

This cemetery is one of the oldest sites in a place that was originally called Old Cottage Grove. The cemetery was founded in 1856, just a few years after the founding of the town itself. Originally, the cemetery was a mere 6 acres as compared to the 32 acres it is today.

Today, there is a white caretaker shed within the grounds of the cemetery. Originally, the white building was completely separate from the cemetery and was called the Lyceum Hall and was used for a vast variety of things in the early days of the town. It was the area's first library. It was used as a community center, and, for the first 17 years of its existence, it was the town hall of Old Cottage Grove. Today, it is just a building used to store tools and equipment for the caretaker of the cemetery.

ghost story

Apparently, the ghosts from this cemetery's long history still inhabit this place. Throughout the cemetery, people sometimes smell remnants of perfume. Perhaps these smells are indications that some female entity is still roaming these grounds. Other times, people hear footsteps falling in the grass behind and around them. When they turn to see who is walking there, there is no one else anywhere in the cemetery.

The white caretaker's shed near the back of the cemetery is also haunted. People see figures looking out through the windows when the building is supposedly empty. Perhaps these figures are remnants of the people who spent so much time in this building when it was still a central structure in the town's early history.

visiting

The ghostly activity that happens in this cemetery has been primarily reported during daylight hours. Due to this fact, your best chance of encountering the ghosts here is during the day. At the time this book was written, there were no hours posted at the cemetery, but you cannot enter once the gates have closed. Typically, the gates are closed near dusk, but this could change depending upon the availability of the caretaker and the season.

EAST IMMANUEL LUTHERAN CHURCH

207 120th Street, Amery, Wisconsin 54001

directions

Take I-35E North from downtown St. Paul for about 4 miles to exit 111A, toward Stillwater. Turn right onto Chestnut Street and follow it for about 23 miles. The road will change names several times and take you into Wisconsin on WI-64 and WI-35. You will then turn left onto WI-46 and follow that for 7 miles to 20th Avenue. Follow 20th Avenue for a mile and then turn right onto 120th Street. The church will be on your left.

history

Nothing incredibly tragic seems to have ever happened within this church. In fact, it seems almost the opposite. Since this Norwegian church was constructed in 1870, countless people have spent some of the happiest and most fulfilling parts of their lives within these walls. In the late 1800s especially, church was a central part of people's lives, especially in rural and remote areas such as this. Perhaps the ghosts here are just reminders of all of the emotions and faith that parishioners exhibited here over the last century and a half.

ghost story

At night, when the sanctuary is completely empty, people sometimes hear the sounds of a congregation murmuring. These murmurs slowly rise in volume and clarity until the witnesses are certain they are hearing people laughing and talking within the sanctuary even though they realize that it's impossible. Sometimes, they even check, and there is no one inside. These sounds of a phantom congregation extend to the basement as well. People hear sounds of a party in the basement but find the basement empty when they check.

This phantom congregation doesn't always exhibit itself as a group. Sometimes, witnesses hear them one at a time. People outside the church have heard a voice calling out to them from the empty church. Other people have been sitting in a pew inside of the church and have heard an unintelligible whisper coming from directly beside them.

Perhaps the strangest phenomenon that haunts this church involves the bell. The phenomenon first occurred in 1981 as the minister of the church was across the street. The bell started ringing. The minister raced across the street, knowing that the building should be empty and no one should be ringing the bell. After searching the building exhaustively, she found that the building was indeed empty. There was no explanation for the ringing bell. Perhaps it could have been considered an isolated incident that could be ignored, except that it happened again . . . and again. Now, those who frequent the church don't think anything of it when the bell rings on its own.

visiting

It is not a good idea to hang around this property at night. At the time this was written, there are no posted signs that say the adjacent cemetery closes at dark. This doesn't mean that if you are there after dark you will not be asked to leave. There was a break-in at the church in the 1970s, and the parishioners and minister are likely to call the police if there are flashlights bouncing through their cemetery in the dead of night. Feel free to visit the cemetery during daylight hours though, especially when there are no services going on in the building. At this time, you can listen for voices or bells coming from the church. Entering the building should be reserved for those who are there to worship.

FERGUSON CEMETERY

18650 County Road 34, Norwood Young America,
Minnesota 55368

directions

Take I-35W South from Minneapolis for about 4 miles to exit 11, MN-62 West.
Stay on MN-62 West for about 6.5 miles until it changes its name to US-212 West.
Continue to follow US-212 for another 33.5 miles and then turn right onto CR-131.
Follow CR-131 for almost 2 miles and then turn left onto CR-34. The cemetery will
be about a mile down the road on your left. It is surrounded by pine trees, and its
entryway is guarded by a metal gate.

history

The cemetery is from the 1800s and has survived despite the surrounding areas having
been converted into farmland. The most interesting facet about the cemetery itself is a
single gravestone that sits alone in the southwest corner of the place. The gravestone is
by far the most isolated stone in the cemetery and is the grave of a young boy.

The reason a young boy would be buried all alone in a remote corner of a
remote cemetery has been lost to history, but from the stories, perhaps it is best that
he is left alone.

ghost story

The cemetery itself is creepy. Many people who wander into this cemetery out in the middle of nowhere feel unwelcome when they are inside the gates. They feel as if there is some strange force within the cemetery trying to get them out. This feeling intensifies the closer you get to the little boy's grave in the southwest corner of the cemetery. Others get the distinct sensation they are being watched, although there is no one else in the area as far as they can see.

Something else that occurs during all times of the day and night is that people see black dogs congregate around the young boy's grave. When approached, even though they seem menacing at first, the dogs disperse and disappear into the trees that line the fence.

Sometimes, the little boy himself is seen within the cemetery. He always appears menacing, glaring at those who see him as if he is about to attack. He always vanishes or darts away before anyone gets close to him.

Perhaps the most famous (and definitely the strangest) ghost story that comes from this cemetery involves a grove of trees situated at the center of the graveyard. According to the story, if you count the number of trees coming out of the ground in that grove before visiting the boy's grave, you will get a different number than when you count them after visiting the boy's grave. Yes, strangely enough, the number of trees in the cemetery supposedly changes every time you walk to the secluded southwest corner of the cemetery.

visiting

The cemetery is quite secluded. It is unlikely that if you go there late at night, you will encounter another person while you're there. At the time this book was written, there were no signs or warnings that the cemetery closes at dusk, and we were unable to find any indications suggesting as much. So, as far as we can tell, the cemetery is open throughout the night. While the ghost stories have been said to happen at any time of the day or night, cemeteries are always creepier at night.

There is nowhere to park along County Road 34, so you will actually need to pull down a dirt road that runs down the west side of the cemetery in order to park.

GREEN LAWN CEMETERY

39864 County Road 20, St Peter, Minnesota 56082

directions

Take I-35W South from downtown Minneapolis for a little more than 7 miles until you reach I-494 West. Follow I-494 West for about 5 miles until you reach US-169 South, exit 10B. Follow US-169 South for 52 miles until you reach Dodd Road. Turn right onto Dodd Road and follow it for about a mile and a half. Turn right onto County Road 20 and follow that for a little more than a mile. The cemetery will be on your right.

history

This cemetery is one of the older ones in the entire state. It was originally organized in March of 1856 by the towns of Traverse des Sioux and St. Peter. Many of the area's most important early settlers were buried here. Not only were the pioneers who first settled this area in the mid-1800s buried here, but the early missionaries who worked with the local Native Americans are also here. The historical sign that greets you as you approach the cemetery also suggests that Civil War veterans are buried here.

The cemetery is no longer in use and has become somewhat decrepit. Broken headstones are stacked haphazardly in a remote corner of the cemetery. Trees and grass have overgrown some of the headstones, and leaves are left unraked. Due to the remoteness of this cemetery, rumors have begun circulating about satanic ceremonies that occur here at night. There is talk about locals who gather here and chant throughout the night, sometimes sacrificing small animals during these rituals.

ghost story

The most often reported phenomenon at Green Lawn Cemetery is that people feel like they are being watched. People often walk into the cemetery and need to leave immediately because they feel a variety of unseen presences watching them.

These intangible feelings aren't the only things that are reported here though. A handful of paranormal investigative groups have been directed to this cemetery by locals who are convinced that it is haunted. These locals say they see dark figures lurking in the cemetery at night and sometimes hear sourceless chanting emanating from the grounds. Paranormal investigation groups have captured strange photos of blurs and shadows on the grounds of the cemetery as well as strange voices on audio recorders that weren't heard at the time of the recording.

visiting

A sign at the entrance to the cemetery informs you that the cemetery closes at dusk. This means that you are unable to enter the cemetery after night has fallen without express permission from the cemetery association, which is unlikely to grant this permission to anyone looking for ghosts. This doesn't mean that this place is impossible to visit to look for ghosts though. It is exceedingly creepy at all times of the day, and many unusual photographs and sounds have been collected by ghost hunters who entered the cemetery at dusk just before it closed.

GREY CLOUD ISLAND CEMETERY

5300 Pioneer Road South, Grey Cloud Island,
Minnesota 55071

directions

From downtown St. Paul, take Warner Road to US-10 East and follow US-10 for 7 miles. Take the County Road 22 exit and turn right onto Summit Avenue. Take the first right onto St. Paul Park Road and then the first left onto Third Street. Follow Third Street for about 2.5 miles. It will change its name to Grey Cloud Island Drive South. Turn left onto Pioneer Road South. On your left, you'll see a large field. At the end of the field you will come to a wooded area. Walk between the edge of the field and the edge of the forest to arrive at the cemetery at the back of the field. It is incredibly difficult to find.

history

This cemetery was originally called Old County Line Cemetery, and it accepted its first burial in 1873. The first person to be buried in the cemetery was an infant child with the name McCoy, who died on February 9 of that year. Due to the history of Grey Cloud Island itself, many of those buried in this particular cemetery are from both Native American and European descent. When the Dakota settlement on the island was forced to move westward, the existing buildings on the island were occupied by traders who had married Native American women. As a result, the cemetery itself is somewhat of a melting pot of the two cultures.

Today, the cemetery seems old and decaying. It is secluded and will often get overgrown. There is a pile of discarded headstones just outside of the cemetery fence. Perhaps these stones are the victims of time or perhaps they are the victims of the vandals who once frequented this cemetery, forcing authorities to make the rule that the cemetery closes after night falls.

ghost story

The cemetery closes at dusk. There seems to be at least one spirit who enforces this rule. At night, people see a figure standing just outside of the gates of the cemetery. He watches anyone who approaches and simply leans against one of the fence posts and smokes a cigarette. Those who watch the figure long enough witness him dissipate into the night.

There are other ghosts that seem to inhabit this small cemetery during the day as well. Some witnesses see a woman hunched over a grave inside of the cemetery. As the witness gets nearer to the woman, she suddenly vanishes. Upon further investigation, the gravestone that she was hunched over marks the grave of an infant child. Other people hear footsteps throughout the cemetery, despite there being no one else there. Others feel unwelcome and uncomfortable while inside the cemetery grounds. Perhaps the ghostly sentry with the cigarette watches visitors even during the day.

visiting

It is very important that you are not in this cemetery after nightfall. Residents on Grey Cloud Island do not like ghost hunters on their island. This is mostly due to the fact that since the ghost stories started circulating about the island, instances of vandalism have increased. The ghost who guards the cemetery at night is seen by people who drive down the adjacent road and glance over at the cemetery on nights when the moon is bright. The cemetery is a little more than a hundred yards from the road but sometimes you can see the figure at night.

During the day, though, you are welcome to explore the cemetery to your heart's content. There is not a parking area for the cemetery. You have to find a place where you can legally park your car alongside the road and then walk to the cemetery. While doing so, make sure you stay off anything that is marked as private property.

HASTINGS STATE ASYLUM CEMETERY

3805 Thomas Drive, Hastings, Minnesota 55033

directions

Take US-61 South from downtown St. Paul for almost 20 miles until you reach Red Wing Boulevard. Turn left onto Red Wing Boulevard and follow that for a mile before turning left onto Tuttle Drive. Take the first left onto Thomas Drive and follow it until it ends. This is where you'll need to park your car. Just beyond the homes on your right is an abandoned road. This road looks like depressions in the grass, and you will get the impression that you are walking through people's backyards. Follow the road and it will take you straight into the cemetery. There is nothing marking the boundaries of the cemetery itself, but there are markers on the ground.

history

This cemetery is well hidden and long forgotten. While it may seem at this time that modern development has helped to hide the cemetery, the cemetery has always been hidden. Those who occupied it and who kept it up preferred to forget about it.

The cemetery is in the extreme southwest corner of a huge 460-acre plat that was once the property of the Hastings Insane Asylum. The insane asylum was built around 1900, and the huge area was used to farm and to produce dairy products by those held at the asylum. The cemetery itself was used for those who were held at the asylum and passed away. People who died at the asylum were victims of all types of mental illnesses, from schizophrenia to Alzheimer's disease. Later in the life of the hospital, it was used as a tuberculosis sanitarium. Throughout the 1920s, tuberculosis was incurable. Many people succumbed to the disease and were buried in the cemetery.

The hospital itself is currently the Hastings Veterans Home in the other corner of the huge land tract. The cemetery holds more than 900 graves and a few remnants of fence posts.

ghost story

Sometimes figures walk through this cemetery during both the day and night. Sometimes these figures are real people who have wandered into the cemetery to pay their respects or to study this little corner of history. Other figures simply vanish into thin air when approached or slowly dissipate into the atmosphere. Despite the cemetery being hidden and mostly forgotten, there is still some activity here. Both the living and the dead walk these grounds.

Besides these strange apparitions that roam the cemetery at all hours, people have heard and even captured strange voices here. Most of the time, these voices are children's voices. Witnesses hear or capture on audio tape the voices of small children despite no children having been there at the time.

visiting

At the time this book was written, there was no sign signifying there is a cemetery here. The only indications that it is actually a cemetery are the headstones that line the ground. Since there were no signs signifying a cemetery, there were no signs that stated the hours the cemetery is open. So at the time that this book was written, you could enter the cemetery at any point during the day or night. If you enter the cemetery late at night, though, show respect to those who are buried there and those who live in the houses nearby.

HOLY NAME CEMETERY

2030 Holy Name Drive, Wayzata, Minnesota 55391

directions

From downtown Minneapolis, take I-394 West for 6 miles until you reach exit 3, the
US-169 North exit. Follow US-169 North for a little more than a mile until you come
upon the MN-55 exit. Follow MN-55 West for about 5.5 miles and then turn right
onto CR-24 West. After about 2 miles, you'll turn right onto Holy Name Drive, and
the cemetery will be there on the corner across from Holy Name Lake.

history

Holy Name Cemetery is an older cemetery that sits on the western outskirts of the
Twin Cities. Its location is one of the most picturesque around the nearby Lake Holy
Name. The cemetery was created to serve a Catholic church that served mainly
Europeans of Germanic ancestry. It is one of the oldest cemeteries in the area, with
headstones that date back to the time when Wayzata was first settled by Europeans in
the mid-1800s.

ghost story

There are several strange reports circulating about this cemetery. The first is that sometimes people inside the cemetery after dark see what appears to be a car pulling into one of the cemetery's entrances, the headlights lost in translucent fog. Suddenly, the headlights vanish, and there is no sign of a vehicle anywhere within the cemetery grounds.

People also encounter odd meteorological phenomena within the cemetery. Outside the gates of the cemetery, it is quite calm and serene. As soon as they enter the cemetery, though, it suddenly becomes violently windy. Upon leaving the cemetery, the weather is back to being calm.

Witnesses have also encountered a white apparition that flits through the cemetery at night. It is always seen at a distance and vanishes before the witnesses can approach it. Others have heard footsteps and voices inside of the cemetery when there is no one talking there.

visiting

This cemetery is open throughout the night, so if you want to enter to try to experience these ghosts, you are able to. If you do enter the cemetery after dark, make sure you exercise the utmost respect for the property. Not only are you standing upon sacred ground, but there are residential houses throughout the area. If people make a commotion in a cemetery after dark and the locals complain, they may soon post signs that close the cemetery at dark. Be respectful so you don't ruin it for the rest of us.

LAKEWOOD CEMETERY MAUSOLEUM

3600 Hennepin Avenue, Minneapolis, Minnesota 55408

directions

From downtown Minneapolis, take I-35W South until you reach exit 14, 35th and 36th Streets. At the end of the exit ramp, turn right onto 35th Street. Take the second left onto Nicollet Avenue South and then the first right onto 36th Street. Follow 36th Street for a mile. Lakewood Cemetery will be on your left just before you reach Lake Calhoun. The mausoleum is an immense two-story structure within the cemetery, near the entrance.

history

Although the cemetery itself has been around since 1872, the mausoleum was built in 1956. It is an immense structure with enough room to fit 3,000 bodies as well as 2,400 urns for cremated remains. It is not known who the ghosts here are or why they choose to haunt this mausoleum. Since the descriptions of them are so diverse, perhaps these ghosts are remnants of those countless bodies interred here.

ghost story

The most haunted location at Lakewood is the large two-story mausoleum. Many stories circulate about ghosts here. People see figures in early 20th-century clothing walking through the hallways of this massive building. These figures seem to be mourning something and won't look up at you even when approached. These figures often vanish as soon as you turn your back on them. Once, an employee at the mausoleum encountered one of these figures, a young woman, in a hallway after closing time. The employee thought the building was empty, so was surprised to find anyone there. The figure said, "I'm looking for my mother." Still confused, the employee turned around to try to get a sense of where this woman came from. When the employee turned back around, the figure had vanished. Despite an exhaustive search of the building, no trace of the woman was ever found.

Strange sounds occur within the mausoleum and throughout the cemetery. People hear metal clanging as if a loose gate were blowing in the wind. People hear footsteps and distant talking within the mausoleum, but the source of these sounds is never found. One account even reports the sounds of drums beating in the distance, but again the source was never found.

visiting

The mausoleum is open every day of the week from 10 a.m. to 4:30 p.m. These are the only times that you are able to enter the mausoleum. Keep in mind that this is a cemetery, so you should exercise the utmost respect when walking through the cemetery grounds. One strange rule that is worth mentioning about the cemetery is that it does not allow photography of any kind. You are not allowed to take any pictures inside the cemetery gates, so if you do happen upon one of the figures in the mausoleum, you won't be able to take his or her picture.

LONG LAKE (UNION) CEMETERY

1314 West Wayzata Boulevard, Long Lake, Minnesota 55356

directions

Take I-394 West from downtown Minneapolis for about 9.5 miles to the end of the Interstate. Exit to the left onto US-12 and follow US-12 for an additional 4.5 miles. Exit US-12 onto Wayzata Boulevard West. A little more than a mile down the road, the cemetery will be on your right on the shore of Long Lake.

history

In the mid-1800s, the area where Union Cemetery sits today was a potential powder keg. Three groups of people were at odds with one another. The actual place where Union Cemetery is today was a hill called Teepee Hill, which served as an encampment for the Chippewa who occupied the area at the time. The Chippewa were at odds with another group of Native Americans called the Dakota, who were also scouting through the area. The third group of people in Long Lake at the time were the European settlers, who had just started to settle in the area.

The European settlers did not have enough military force at their disposal to drive the potentially dangerous Chippewa from the area, so they devised a scheme to move the Chippewa from the land. Since the Dakota and the Chippewa were unfriendly with one another, the settlers decided they would try to spark a war between the two tribes. The settlers revealed to the Dakota the location of Teepee Hill, where the Chippewa were based, and then informed the Chippewa that the Dakota were in the area and knew where they were. As a result, the Chippewa were forced to vacate the area to a safer place until the potential hostilities were calmed.

In the meantime, the settlers turned Teepee Hill into a cemetery, knowing that if the Chippewa ever returned they would be unwilling to encamp upon sacred ground.

ghost story

At night, people hear voices coming from the cemetery. The words are never discernible; it is almost as if they are speaking a different language. Whenever these voices are investigated, no source is ever found. Eventually, the voices just fade away, and the witness wonders whether they were ever really there in the first place.

These phantom voices aren't the only things that haunt this cemetery. People who are on the lake or across the lake at night report seeing what looks like a series of campfires burning in the area that is today the cemetery. Confused, the witnesses will sometimes go closer to investigate, but the closer they get to the cemetery, the more these mysterious campfires seem to fade away. Strangely, these campfires are only seen by those looking out across the water.

visiting

The cemetery closes at dusk, but this is not a problem. Even though the ghostly activity here is experienced exclusively at night, it is always experienced by someone outside of the cemetery. Those who happen to be near the cemetery at night but not inside hear the voices, and those who are looking across water have seen the campfires. The campfires are seen most often from out on the lake itself or from the small peninsula that juts into the lake directly across from the cemetery. Unfortunately, there is no easy access to this peninsula from land. Your best bet is to either go out on the lake or find a vantage point where you can look out across the water and still see the cemetery.

MARIAN CENTER

200 Earl Street, St. Paul, Minnesota 55106

directions

From downtown St. Paul, take Kellogg Avenue to the east for a mile until you get to Mounds Boulevard. Turn right onto Mounds Boulevard and follow it for about a mile until you reach Earl Street. Turn left onto Earl Street, and the Marian Center will be on your right at the first intersection.

history

The original building at the site was built in 1910 and was known as the Mounds Park Sanitarium. Medical practices in the early 1900s were primitive at best, and many people who would have easily survived illness today died in the hospital because of the lack of medical knowledge. As time went on, though, medical practices slowly improved, and this hospital was regarded as one of the best in the area. The name was changed to Mounds Park Hospital.

By the 1980s, health care was improving and rapidly changing in the St. Paul area. The Mounds Park Hospital was getting too big for the building in which it was confined. The hospital moved and combined with other hospitals in the area, leaving the building temporarily vacant. In 1989, a nursing home known as the Marian Center of St. Paul took over the building and has operated there since.

During the time when the building was abandoned, security guards often patrolled the old hospital. One night a security guard was doing a sweep of the building and took an elevator down to the basement where the morgue once was. When the doors to the elevator opened, he was surprised by trespassers and was shot dead.

ghost story

The basement and the old morgue are the most haunted places in this building. Many employees at the Marian Center will not go into the basement despite the fact that their break area is down there. When walking through the empty basement at night, strange sounds come from the morgue despite the fact that there is no one there. Metallic scraping, banging, and footsteps are all heard coming from the empty basement.

One of the elevators in the building seems to be possessed by some sort of entity in the basement as well. Despite what floor you are trying to go to, when you hit the button for that floor, the elevator takes you to the basement. The doors open, revealing the basement and the abandoned morgue, and then close and take you to the floor you had originally intended to visit.

visiting

Unfortunately, the ghosts here are incredibly difficult to visit. The building is still an operational nursing home, and many people live and work here. Often, the last things on their minds are the ghosts in the basement. In order to visit this place, and perhaps experience the ghosts in the basement, you almost have to be an employee or a resident here. Otherwise, you may just have to admire the haunted building from the outside.

MEMORIAL PET CEMETERY
694 Cope Avenue, Roseville, Minnesota

directions
Take I-35W North from downtown Minneapolis for about 4.5 miles to exit 23B, the MN-36 East exit. Follow MN-36 East for 3 more miles before taking the Dale Street exit. At the end of the exit ramp, turn left onto Dale Street and then take the first left after the highway onto Cope Avenue. The pet cemetery will be on your left.

history
In the early 1920s, a man sold off a few acres of his farm to a local veterinarian named Dr. Feist, who immediately turned the area into the first pet cemetery in Minnesota. It was originally called the Feist Pet Cemetery and was privately owned until the late 1980s when it was donated to the local Humane Society and was renamed Memorial Pet Cemetery.

Throughout its many years of existence, a vast variety of animals have been buried here—mostly dogs. The headstones themselves often mention what type of dog it was and include a touching epitaph. Dogs aren't the only pets buried here though. There are birds, hamsters, gerbils, cats, and even a horse. The horse's grave is currently unmarked, and historic records as to its exact location have been lost. A human is also buried in the cemetery. A woman asked the current owner of the cemetery if it was okay if her ashes were buried with her pet dog. After searching through current laws and regulations, the owner agreed to allow it, and her ashes were buried with her beloved pet.

Today, there is no longer any room in the cemetery, and no new burials are being accepted.

ghost story

While you might expect a pet cemetery to be haunted by the spirits of the animals buried here, most of the ghost stories actually involve human entities. Every once in a while, people hear what sounds like a quiet barking of a dog or a rustling through the grass, but the dogs from the local neighborhood or resident squirrels could account for these phenomena.

The most often-seen ghost in the cemetery is that of a small boy. People encounter a small boy who is alone within the cemetery. Often the witnesses see him in a particular place, but when they go off exploring and then turn back to look at the little boy, he has completely vanished. Other times, those who see this young boy say the boy follows them around the cemetery at a safe distance and then suddenly disappears. Still others hear the voice of a small boy, although they do not see the boy anywhere.

The other ghost within this cemetery is that of an old woman. The woman is seen kneeling in front of a dog's gravestone. When she is approached, she fades away into nothingness.

visiting

It is best to explore this location during daylight hours. One reason for this is that the cemetery is in a neighborhood and concerned residents may call the police if someone is walking through a pet cemetery in the middle of the night with a flashlight. Perhaps a more important reason to explore here during the day, though, is that all of the ghost stories have been reported by those exploring during the day.

MINNEAPOLIS PIONEERS AND SOLDIERS CEMETERY

2945 Cedar Avenue South, Minneapolis, Minnesota 55407

directions

From downtown Minneapolis, take I-35W South to the MN-55 East ramp. Follow that ramp for a half mile and then take the Cedar Avenue ramp. Turn right onto Cedar Avenue and follow it for about three-quarters of a mile. The cemetery will be on your left.

history

This is the oldest cemetery in Minneapolis, with a long and tumultuous history. The first burial here was in 1853, in the earliest days of Minneapolis. An eclectic group of people is buried here. In the early days of the cemetery, the pioneers who first cleared and settled the area were buried here. Three veterans of the War of 1812 were buried here, and at least 150 Civil War veterans were buried here.

Despite the prestige of many of the early burials in the cemetery, the vast majority of people who are buried here were working class people from the late 1800s and early 1900s. Many of the people who literally built the city were buried here. Many of them couldn't afford to be buried anywhere else and their internments were paid for by the city. Section H is the saddest section: Abandoned infants who died helpless in the streets are buried here. Suicides and other nameless people who were found dead in and around Minneapolis were laid here to rest. Another part of section H contains a mass grave where 355 bodies were dumped after being used by medical students for research.

In 1919, people in the surrounding neighborhoods were concerned about the poor condition of the cemetery and asked that it no longer be used. The city passed an ordinance preventing all further burials. In the 66 years this cemetery accepted burials, at least 22,000 people were buried here. It is estimated that at least 50 percent of the people buried in the cemetery are children under the age of ten.

ghost story

Many people have heard or seen strange things in this cemetery. Figures have been seen slowly walking through the cemetery, looking down at the ground and paying no attention to the world around them. When these figures are approached, they slowly fade away to nothingness. Sometimes these figures are missing body parts such as arms—or even their heads. While these figures are seen throughout the cemetery, they are most often seen near Section H, where the medical research specimens were buried.

While these figures are seen from time to time, the most prolific ghosts here are those of children. Most of the time, these children are heard. People hear an infant crying but will be unable to locate the source of the sounds. Other times, people hear what sound like children playing or a child talking, but no matter how hard they search, they are unable to find the children anywhere in or near the cemetery.

visiting

The cemetery is not open throughout the night, so the only way to visit the ghosts here is to go when it is open. Unfortunately, the hours for the cemetery are very limited. It is only open Wednesday through Sunday, April 15 to October 15. During these times, the cemetery opens at 8 a.m. and closes at 4:30 p.m..

If these hours are too limiting, but you still want to visit the cemetery, you can schedule an appointment with the Department of Public Works by dialing (612) 729-8484.

MONASTERY AT DEMONTREVILLE

8243 DeMontreville Trail North, Lake Elmo,
Minnesota 55042

directions

From St. Paul, take I-35E North for about 4 miles to exit 111A, MN-36 East towards
Stillwater. Follow MN-36 East for 8.5 miles until you reach DeMontreville Trail.
Turn right onto DeMontreville Trail and follow the road for about a mile to get to
the monastery complex. The monastery buildings will be on your left before you
reach the lake.

history

The history of the buildings in this monastery complex is by no means long. The Jesuit
retreat and monastery were not built until 1987, and there are several buildings within

the complex. This is an actual Jesuit monastery, where the monks live a life of prayer and silence. There is a retreat house where people come to find themselves. There is also a building where nuns live in silence and solitude as well.

The complex has no dark history associated with it. The location of the buildings was chosen because it was so far away from civilization, and the monks wanted to live with a sense of isolation from the rest of the world and focus on their faith.

ghost story

The ghost at the monastery does not haunt the buildings themselves but the road that runs directly adjacent to the monastery. While the story itself may sound somewhat like an urban legend, there are many witnesses to this particular spirit who adamantly claim otherwise.

This ghost supposedly only appears between midnight and 1 a.m. The story goes that if a car is driving down the road during this time, a monk dressed in brown robes will run out into the street directly in front of the car. The monk is thin and young, in his 20s or early 30s. The cars that witness this apparition are unable to stop in time. Luckily, the apparition vanishes into thin air just as the car passes through him.

visiting

This is an easy ghost to attempt to experience. Since the road adjacent to the monastery is open to the public throughout the night, there are no legal restrictions to driving up and down the road as much as you like and at whatever time you like. Another thing that makes witnessing this apparition easy is the fact that the ghost only appears at a specific time of night. Still, be considerate as you drive by since monks are sleeping or meditating nearby.

If you're driving down the road and a man in a brown robe jumps in front of your car, still try to stop. The monastery is still an active monastery with monks who live inside. You wouldn't want to hit a living person.

OAKLAND CEMETERY

927 Jackson Street, St. Paul, Minnesota 55117

directions

Take Jackson Street from the heart of downtown St. Paul away from the river for a little less than a mile. The cemetery will be on your left. It takes up ten blocks between Sycamore Street and Magnolia Street.

history

Oakland Cemetery has existed since 1853 and was the first nondenominational cemetery in Minnesota. Since the time of its creation, the cemetery has grown, assimilating other nearby cemeteries and expanding physically to over 100 acres. Throughout its long life, more than 50,000 people have been buried here, including Civil War soldiers, area firefighters, and many famous people from the area's early history, like writer and educator Harriet Bishop and Alexander Ramsey, one of the first mayors of St. Paul and the second governor of Minnesota.

It's hard to say who the ghost at Oakland Cemetery might be. Throughout the years, so many people have been buried here, many dying before their time, that pinpointing the exact spirit that has been left behind is nearly impossible.

ghost story

While no one knows who haunts this historic cemetery, many have seen her, and they all describe her exactly the same way. They see the apparition of a woman walking through the cemetery. Sometimes she simply roams the cemetery for a while before mysteriously vanishing. Other times, the apparition actually approaches witnesses before disappearing before their eyes.

Perhaps the strangest thing about this apparition is that she is described exactly the same by most all who see her. She is a young woman who appears to be somewhere around the age of 25. She stands somewhere between 5'5" and 5'7" tall. She has straight brown hair that falls to about her shoulders, and she is always wearing a long white dress with lace lining the edges. Even those witnesses who have never heard the stories of this woman still describe her exactly this way.

visiting

This cemetery can only be entered during regular business hours. The cemetery is open during different hours during the summer than it is during the winter. During the summer, it is open from 8 a.m. until 8 p.m., and during the winter it is open from 8 a.m. until 4:30 p.m. Do not try to enter the cemetery outside of these hours, or you will be arrested and fined. The ghost is seen during regular visiting hours in secluded sections of the cemetery. So if you want to see her, make your way to a secluded section of the grounds and perhaps you'll run into her.

OXLIP EVANGELICAL FREE CHURCH

4770 County Road 5 NW, Isanti, Minnesota 55040

directions

From downtown Minneapolis, take I-94 West for about 4.5 miles to MN-252 North. Take MN-252 North for about 4 miles until you reach MN-610 East. Follow MN-610 East for about 3 miles to the Round Lake Boulevard exit. Turn right onto Round Lake Boulevard and follow it for about 13 miles. Halfway through, its name changes to Lake George Boulevard. Turn left onto Bridge Street and then right onto Ambassador Boulevard less than a mile later. Take the second right onto St. Francis Boulevard and follow that for 7 miles. Turn left onto County Road 5. After a mile, the church will be on your left

history

Before there was a church here, there was farmland. In the 1800s, a farmer worked this land and hired a farmhand to help him with the hard work. At some point, the farmer and the farmhand began fighting about something. A few days later, the farmhand was found dead near where the church is today.

The history of the church building itself goes back to the early 1900s when two small Swedish Mission churches combined into one building on the site. This building was the entirety of this church for about 80 years. In 1980, a huge addition was added to the original Swedish Missions. This addition completed the church as it stands today.

Throughout the years, many people have come and gone through these doors to worship or for community gatherings. Sometimes, the church houses homeless people during the brutal Minnesota winters. This building has been a center of warmth and faith for more than a hundred years.

ghost story

Strange things happen in the basement of this church. The paranormal phenomenon that occurs most frequently is people hearing footsteps following them around in the basement. People staying the night in the basement sometimes get up in the middle of the night to use the restroom or the kitchen, and as they are walking through the building in the dark, they hear someone walking behind them. They turn around but find no one else is awake in the entire building.

Strange plumbing and electrical things also happen in the basement. Lights flicker on and off in the middle of the night. Faucets slowly turn on until they are on full force and then suddenly shut off as if they were never on to begin with.

Strange things happen on the church grounds as well. People see the farmhand who had been killed walking aimlessly before disappearing. Another story tells about a woman who walks the grounds looking for something. Those who are aware of the ghost of the woman say that she is searching for a lost child who had been taken away.

visiting

Staying the night in the basement of this church is typically not an option for those of us who are trying to find ghosts in this building. Your best bet as an outsider wanting to find some evidence of ghostly activity in this building is to drive by late at night. The phenomenon you might be able to see at this time is the lights in the basement flickering on and off.

On the other hand, the ghosts outside the church are visible to outsiders. These ghosts typically manifest late at night. Feel free to watch for them all night long. Just make sure that you are not trespassing on church property.

RAMSEY COUNTY POOR FARM CEMETERY

2000 White Bear Avenue, Maplewood, Minnesota 55109

directions

From downtown St. Paul, take I-35E North for about 4 miles until you reach MN-36 East at exit 111A towards Stillwater. Follow MN-36 East for a little more than 3 miles to the White Bear Avenue exit. Turn right at the end of the exit ramp, and the cemetery will be just past Burke Avenue on your left. The cemetery is actually a small park with sidewalks crossing through it just before you get to the horseshoe courts.

history

The Poor Farm Cemetery was established in 1893 as one of the first cemeteries for the indigent in the state. Throughout the years that the cemetery accepted burials, 1894 to 1923, more than 3,000 people were buried here. Most of them were poor. When they died, they did not have the money to afford burial in any of the other cemeteries in the area, and they did not know anyone who would fund a proper burial in another cemetery. About a tenth of the cemetery is populated by those people who were never claimed by anyone. Abandoned infants, homeless people found near rail lines, and suicides make up a significant portion of the people who were buried here.

As the 20th century drew to a close, the cemetery was in danger of disappearing. Portions of the edges of the cemetery were taken over by other things. The Ramsey County Fairgrounds built a racetrack on the east side of the cemetery. White Bear Avenue was built over the west side of the cemetery. Horseshoe courts were built to the south, and a pipeline was placed to the north of the cemetery. In 2001, the Maplewood Area Historical Society was able to convince the county to preserve the remainder of the cemetery. The county funded the area so that it would be preserved as a heritage park.

ghost story

There seems to be paranormal activity here at the cemetery during all times of the day and night. The most frequently reported ghost here involves the sounds of footsteps. People standing in the cemetery alone often hear what sounds like a person walking around nearby. Despite exhaustive searching, no one is ever found.

There are also strange temperature fluctuations reported, especially near the woods on the north side of the cemetery. The temperature suddenly drops significantly and then quickly rises again to where it was originally.

Figures and voices also are seen and heard throughout the cemetery. Shadowy figures are seen throughout the cemetery but fade away or suddenly vanish. Sometimes people hear voices that seem like they are coming from a distance. The source of these voices is never discovered. Other times, witnesses hear what sounds like an infant crying.

visiting

At the time this book was written, there was nothing at the cemetery that suggests it closes at dark. The paranormal happenings seem to occur both during the day and night, but it is always creepier to approach a haunted location after the sun sets. If you do enter the park after dark, look to make sure nothing is posted that suggests the rules have changed and it does now actually close at dark.

While there isn't a certain time of the day or night where there are more reports of paranormal activity, there is a section of the cemetery that seems to be more haunted. Your best chance for finding ghosts here is to go to the north side of the cemetery near the woods.

ST. PAUL CATHEDRAL

239 Selby Avenue, St. Paul, Minnesota 55102

directions

Take Kellogg Boulevard in the heart of downtown St. Paul to the west until you get to John Ireland Boulevard and turn left. You will be unable to miss the magnificent cathedral looming powerfully above. The entrance is the third right on Selby Avenue.

history

The construction of this vast and beautiful building was an incredibly long process that began in 1904. Archbishop John Ireland was able to purchase the highest point in the city to use as the site of his magnificent cathedral. The cornerstone was not placed until three years later in June of 1907. It took another eight years until the building was complete enough to begin holding mass. Construction would continue for quite some time after this. It wasn't until the fall of 1958 that the building was finally complete. The excessive amount of work was worth it. The cathedral dominates the city from the hill. Anyone who sees it cannot help but be filled with a sense of awe.

Throughout the many years this building has been in existence, it has seen its share of emotion. In addition to those who would spend almost every day worshipping here, it has been the site of many funerals. Perhaps some remnant of all of this history and emotion has lived on the cathedral.

ghost story

Often, when visitors enter this sacred building, they feel they are not alone. These visitors always have a sense that there are people within the building and in the pews that they cannot see. Sometimes witnesses encounter cold spots when they sit down in an empty pew. Other times the pews creak as if someone is sitting in them and shifting their weight, although there is no one there. Other times sounds like footsteps or coughs will echo throughout the building although their source cannot be found.

These vague encounters with spirits in the cathedral almost seem as if they are a trick of the senses in a place as large and full of echoes as this, if it weren't for the other paranormal instance that has happened here a couple of times. When tourists take photographs of the empty pews, sometimes something strange appears in the pictures. Wispy, white figures often show up in the pictures despite the pews having been empty at the time the pictures were taken.

visiting

The cathedral is not only a place of worship but is also a tourist destination because of its magnificent architecture and art. There is actually a gift shop inside of the building. The cathedral is open to the public Sunday through Friday from 7 a.m. until 7 p.m. On Saturday, the building is open from 7 a.m. until 9 p.m. During regular hours, you are welcome to walk through the building and explore. There are pamphlets in the gift shop offering a self-guided tour of the building. The only times that you cannot explore at will is during mass times, which are constantly subject to change. Since this building is a place of worship, make sure you approach your exploration with utmost respect. You are permitted to take photographs inside of the building as long as there is not a mass going on at the time.

VANG LUTHERAN CHURCH

2060 County 49 Boulevard, Dennison, Minnesota 55053

directions

Take US-52 South from downtown St. Paul for about 25 miles until you reach the MN-50 exit towards MN-56. Merge onto MN-56 South and follow that for another 17 miles. Turn right onto County 49 Boulevard and follow that for another mile. Vang Lutheran Church will be on your left.

history

The haunted history of this place does not have anything to do with any kind of tragedy. It is more likely to do with the age of the building itself. The church has been around for more than 170 years and has been in constant operation during that time. Many people have worshipped in this building throughout its long history. Weddings and funerals have occurred here. Since this building has been a central location in the faith of many people over the many years of its existence, it is no wonder that some sort of energy or spirits have made their imprint upon this place.

ghost story

Specifically, what makes this location a famous paranormal hot spot is a single photograph that was taken in the late 1930s. While nothing was seen or experienced at the time the photograph was taken, later examination of the photo shows a ghost. An out-of-focus specter is seen crossing the church towards the basement steps. The photograph has never been explained.

This strange photo isn't the only thing that has been experienced here though. Voices are often heard echoing throughout the church even when there is no one talking. Those who are alone in the church when they hear these voices search fruitlessly for the source of these phantom sounds but never find anything that could explain them. The voices are rarely clear enough to decipher what they are saying. Those who hear them can only tell they are strange voices that have no discernible source.

visiting

This haunted location is rather difficult for an outsider to visit. This is an actual church that is still in operation. Those who worship there and who run the place do not want ghost enthusiasts constantly moving through their building looking for ghosts. The building itself is beautiful. Feel free to join the congregation for one of their services and perhaps keep a close ear out for some voices that may be from the great beyond.

SECTION III

museums, shops, and entertainment

AMF EARLE BROWN BOWL

6440 James Circle North, Brooklyn Park, Minnesota 56715

directions

From downtown Minneapolis, take I-94 West for about 5.5 miles to exit 34, the Shingle Creek Parkway exit. Turn left onto Shingle Creek Parkway and then take the first left onto Freeway Boulevard. Take the first right onto James Circle North. The bowling alley will be on your left.

history

For a while the building was simply called the AMF Bowling Lanes, but in 2005 these lanes went out of business, and the building was boarded up. The next year, the AMF Earle Brown Bowl was built and has continued to operate as a bowling alley since.

When the alley was simply the AMF Bowling Lanes, there was a bowler who spent at least some time every day at the lanes. Those who knew him knew that bowling was the most important thing in his life, and that he would stop at nothing to perfect his game. One day, while at home, he unexpectedly died. Some say this didn't stop him from coming back to the bowling alley.

ghost story

Some of the employees at the bowling alley laugh when you mention the ghost here. It isn't necessarily a frightening ghost, but it is a ghost everyone knows about but few people really talk about. The lanes sometimes switch on and off by themselves. Perhaps the avid bowler who passed away is trying to switch on a lane so he can play. Other strange things happen throughout the building during the course of the business day. Items move by themselves. Drinks fall over despite no one being near them. The electronics on some of the lanes malfunction all of a sudden.

Despite little things like this happening at the bowling alley during business hours, stranger things sometimes occur there after it closes. Once the building is completely closed down and empty for the night, people still hear the sounds of bowling balls rolling down the alley and pins falling.

visiting

You have a couple options if you want to encounter this particular ghost. First, you can enter the bowling alley during business hours and maybe experience one of the strange happenings that occur there. The alley opens at 9 a.m. every day of the week except Sunday, when it opens at 10 a.m., and closes at 11 p.m. every day of the week except Thursday, Friday, and Saturday when it closes at 1 a.m. Your other option is to stand outside of the bowling alley long after it has closed, when you might hear the ghostly bowler perfecting his game in the middle of the night.

ANOKA COUNTY HISTORICAL SOCIETY

2135 Third Avenue North, Anoka, Minnesota 55303

directions

From downtown Minneapolis, take I-94 North for about 4.5 miles to MN-252 North. Follow MN-252 for another 4 miles and then merge onto MN-610 West. Follow MN-610 for about 4.5 more miles and then merge onto US-169 North. Follow US-169 for 5 miles and then turn right onto Main Street. After about a quarter mile, turn left onto N. Third Avenue. The historical society building will be on your left. There is a parking lot in front of the building.

history

Given the long history of Anoka itself, the building that currently houses the historical society museum and library is quite young. The building was constructed in 1971, and the historical society moved there from Colonial Hall in 1972.

Due to its young age, the building lacks tragedy. No one has died within the building. It does contain a large amount of historic artifacts and documents though. Perhaps someone, or something, has attached itself to the documents housed here.

ghost story

Some ghosts make themselves known quite often in this building. Librarians and visitors to the historical society library see shadowy figures lurking near the edges of the bookshelves. When these figures are investigated, there is no one there and no one anywhere nearby. People also often hear phantom footsteps within the building, which echo through the building when it is supposedly empty. Other times, witnesses approach the supposed source of these footsteps and find no one nearby.

These figures and sounds are not the only things that haunt this place though. Once, an archivist was working in the building in the morning before it opened, and she heard the chime of the front door. Assuming that it was the delivery person, she went upstairs only to find the building empty. This happened a second time the same morning. The front door has a pressure pad that registers anyone who enters the building. When the archivist checked the counter on the pad, it had registered that two people had entered the building.

Another time, a visitor was inside the building researching her family's genealogy when suddenly a book dropped from a shelf behind her. When she walked to the book to replace it, she noticed that the book was lying open to a page that detailed her own family's history.

visiting

In order to enter the building and experience these ghosts for yourself, you need to enter during the time when they are open. The building is open on Tuesday from 10 a.m.–8 p.m., and on Wednesday through Friday from 10 a.m.–5 p.m. On Saturday, the building is open from 10 a.m.–4 p.m., and it is closed Sunday and Monday. You do have another opportunity to hear the stories from directly outside of the historical society building. Every Thursday and Saturday in October, the historical society offers a ghost tour of Anoka, which details some stories about the building. It is at 7:30 p.m. and costs adults $7 to attend.

ANTIQUES ON MAIN

212 East Main Street, Anoka, Minnesota 55303

directions

From downtown Minneapolis, take I-94 North for about 4.5 miles to MN-252 North. Follow MN-252 for another 4 miles and then merge onto MN-610 West. Follow MN-610 for about 4.5 more miles and then merge onto US-169 North. Follow US-169 for 5 miles and then turn right onto Main Street. Antiques on Main will be on your right.

history

The buildings along Main Street in Anoka are all more than 100 years old. Many shops have occupied these buildings throughout the years, and many people have owned or have visited stores here. Perhaps any paranormal activity in these places is just a remnant of those who have spent so much time in these buildings during their long history.

The actual space where Antiques on Main is currently was once a furniture store. Since it was the only furniture-building establishment in town, much of the town's furniture and other wooden necessities were built at the store. In the early days of the town, this also included coffins. Many of the coffins used for people in Anoka were built within the store.

ghost story

Antiques on Main seems to be haunted by the ghost of a little boy. People see figures, especially that of a child, walking throughout the store but especially on the stairs leading to the basement. Once a worker was in the basement and heard shuffling in the room beside her. As she went to investigate, she suddenly heard the sound of a little boy asking, "Grandma, where are you?" Still unable to find the boy, she heard the voice again, "Grandma, where are you? I can't see you."

Besides the figures in the store, items fall from shelves, and people hear the floor creaking as if someone is walking across it only to find no one is there.

visiting

You can enter the store to search for their ghosts any time the building is open for business. It is open every day of the week from 9 a.m.–6 p.m. except for Wednesday and Thursday when it is open until 8 p.m.

ARTIQUE INC.

1900 Third Avenue, Anoka, Minnesota 55303

directions

From downtown Minneapolis, take I-94 West for about 4.5 miles to the MN-252 North exit on the right side of the interstate. Follow MN-252 for about 4 miles to MN-610 West on the left side of the road. After about 4.5 miles on MN-610 West, merge onto US-169 North. Follow US-169 for 5 miles and then turn right onto Main Street. Take the third right onto Third Avenue. The Artique will be on your left near the intersection with Monroe Street.

history

The building where Artique Inc. is held today was originally both a home and clinic built in 1904. Alanson and Flora Aldrich were both doctors who ran an office out of their home on the corner of Third Avenue and Monroe. They ran the clinic for nearly 20 years until they died in the early 1920s.

Eventually, the home passed into the hands of the Anoka Historical Society, which decided to rent the space to Artique Inc., a business that sells both antiques and art. The Artique building is a stop on the historical society's ghost tour every October.

ghost story

Perhaps the countless ill and dying people who frequented the home when it was a clinic haunt this place. Perhaps the ghosts of Alanson and Flora have remained in the home where they spent the last 20 years of their lives. Perhaps the antiques here today have retained some energy from their former owners. Regardless, though, this building is haunted.

From the exterior of the building, people often see the ghost of a woman looking down and waving at passersby. Many assume this is the ghost of Flora, greeting visitors. This ghost also is seen by people inside the building. People see a woman in the upstairs, who either vanishes or who turns a corner and is never seen again.

This friendly ghost is not the only presence in the building. There are other ghosts, but they are more aggressive. People sometimes smell cigar smoke when inside the building despite the fact that no one has smoked a cigar in the building for ages. Others are touched on the hair or on the back by unseen forces. This phenomenon happens most often in the basement. Perhaps the most common paranormal occurrence is things moving throughout the house without any physical reason. Items are thrown by unseen forces from tables or ledges. Things fall off shelves or fall and then roll off tables. Something beyond our understanding is at work in this place.

visiting

In order to experience most of the ghosts here, you will need to enter the building during regular business hours. On every day of the week except Sunday, the store is open from 10 a.m.–5:30 p.m. On Sunday, the store is open from 11 a.m.–5 p.m. During these hours, you can explore the house, check out the merchandise, and maybe encounter one of the ghosts.

After business hours, it is still possible to encounter one of the famous ghosts of this building. At any hour of the day or night, you may see a strange apparition of a woman waving at you from out of a second-floor window. The Anoka Historical Society also runs a ghost tour during October, and they stop at the Artique to tell some of these stories.

CARVER COUNTRY FLOWERS AND GIFTS

109 Third Street East, Carver, Minnesota 55315

directions

From downtown Minneapolis, take I-35W South for about 4 miles to exit 11, the MN-62 West exit. Follow MN-62 for 6.5 miles and follow US-212 West on the left side of the highway. Follow US-212 for about 16 miles and then take the Jonathan Carver Parkway exit. At the end of the ramp, turn left onto Jonathan Carver Parkway and follow the road for a little more than a mile. Turn left onto Sixth Street West and follow it for about a mile before turning right again onto Broadway Street. Take the second left onto Third Street, and the flower shop will be on your right.

history

While the businesses that occupy this building today have not been here very long, the building itself is actually one of the oldest in the area. It was built in 1868, and throughout all the years it was used as retail space for the town of Carver, it retained much of the same floors, walls, and ceilings from the time it was built. Countless stores have occupied the property during its long history. Countless shoppers and owners have walked upon these floors and swept up after closing.

In January of 2000, the building was bought by a husband and wife and used to house their antique store called Treasure Chest Antiques. For the next decade, the husband-and-wife team ran the antique store. In 2008, they rented out some space to Carver Country Flowers and Gifts. In March of 2010, Treasure Chest Antiques relocated to a different building in Jordan, Minnesota, but Carver Country Flowers and Gifts remained here.

ghost story

Despite the fact that most of the ghost stories from this building are from the time when it was still occupied by Treasure Chest Antiques, every once in a while someone still experiences something paranormal here.

The ghostly phenomena that are reported here are primarily sounds. Many times when people are in secluded areas of the store or the building, they hear footsteps. Sometimes these footsteps are in parts of the building that are supposedly completely empty. Other times, the footsteps approach the witnesses and then just fade into nothingness. Some who experience these footsteps dismiss them as the natural settling sounds of the old building, but there is another sound heard here that is harder to explain away. Many times people hear what sounds like someone sweeping the floor with a broom, although there is no one sweeping.

visiting

At the time that this book was written, the building was occupied by two businesses. The older and primary business is the Carver Country Flowers and Gifts store, but there is also an antique shop in the building called The Good Junk Garage. The flower shop is open every day except Sunday from 10 a.m.–5 p.m. It's closed on Sunday. The Good Junk Garage store has more limited hours that frequently change due to the availability of the shop's proprietor. You need to enter the store during regular business hours during a time when it is not busy to experience the ghosts here.

GIBBS FARMHOUSE MUSEUM

2097 Larpenteur Avenue West, St. Paul, Minnesota 55113

directions

From downtown Minneapolis, take I-35W North for about 4.5 miles to exit 23B, the MN-36 East exit. At the end of the ramp, take Cleveland Avenue North and follow this road for about a mile. Turn right onto Larpenteur Avenue West. The Gibbs Farmhouse Museum will be on your right before you get to the golf course entrance.

history

The Gibbs Farmhouse itself was built in 1854 by a man named Herman Gibbs. The family had lived on the property and farmed there since 1849 and had made friends with the local Native Americans who lived in the area. The Gibbs family quickly began to grow and in 1858, little Willie Gibbs was born.

The next nine years carried on rather uneventfully. The family continued to grow as they made their living off of the land. In 1867, though, a brush fire started on their property and started devastating the landscape. The family did what they could to protect the house and what they could of the fields. Little Willie was by then nine years old and was able to aid his family in the protection of the house. After the danger from the fire subsided, the house was saved. Willie, however, had inhaled an amount of smoke during the incident. Within the next few days, Willie was dead.

ghost story

According to many of the witnesses who have experienced activity here, Willie has haunted the house and subsequently the museum since his death in 1867. Within the museum, there are display cabinets filled with some of Willie's toys from the time that he was still alive. Despite the fact that these display cabinets are always locked, toys will from time to time find their way out of the cabinets and onto the floor. This will usually happen at night, and these toys will not be found outside of their cases until the employees open up the building the next morning.

Playing with the toys is not the only thing that Willie does to keep himself occupied. Sometimes people will leave one of the downstairs rooms and will return to find that all of the cabinet doors have been opened despite no one having entered the room. Other times, visitors will hear the rocking chair upstairs rocking back and forth. This will happen when there is no one upstairs.

Willie is also seen from time to time. People outside of the house have looked towards the windows and seen a small boy looking out at them. This will sometimes happen when the building is closed and there is no one inside.

visiting

For most of the ghostly happenings in this building, you will have to enter during regular business hours in order to experience anything. The building is open from noon to 4 every day of the week except Monday, when it's closed. Your best chance of running into a spirit is during this time. Admission is $8 for adults.

If you're not able to make it during normal business hours, or you don't want to pay the $8 admission fee, you may still have a chance to see Willie. Since people have seen Willie in the windows of the house even after it's closed, you can drive up to the house and peer in. Maybe Willie will stop by and say hi.

HILLCREST RECREATION CENTER

1978 Ford Parkway, St. Paul, Minnesota 55116

directions

Take I-35E South from downtown St. Paul for about 3.5 miles to exit 103B, the West Seventh Street exit. At the end of the exit ramp, turn right onto Fort Road. At Montreal Avenue, take a slight right and follow Montreal for about a mile. Turn right onto Snelling Avenue South after you pass the Highland National Golf Course and then turn left onto Ford Parkway. Hillcrest Recreation Center will be on your left just before Kenneth Street.

history

It's hard to tell what facet of this building's history may have generated the ghosts that occupy the top floor. No one died during the construction as it was erected in 1994. As far as archaeologists know, there were no Native American burial mounds or grave sites underneath the building. Throughout the life of the building, no one has died within its walls or even as a direct result of anything that happened within the building. Everything about the building seems normal.

In 1994, the government of St. Paul built the rec center to hold a gym and other sporting and exercise facilities for the surrounding population. The rec center also holds classes and other community educational events.

ghost story

All of the paranormal activity seems to occur on the upper floor of the Hillcrest Recreation Center. The first strange story involves temperature fluctuations. People experience extreme cold spots throughout the upstairs. It feels as if you are standing underneath an air conditioning vent despite the fact that there is no vent close by.

The other story from the upstairs of the building is that people hear laughter even though there is no one nearby laughing. The laughter always comes from a male, and the witnesses often look around in vain trying to find the laughter's source.

visiting

The recreation center is open to the public but can only be entered during regular hours. The building is closed on Saturday and Sunday, but is open at 8:30 a.m. every other day of the week. It is open until 9 p.m. on Monday through Thursday and until 6 p.m. on Friday. Many of the sports and activities at the rec center have a fee, but you should have no problem walking into the upstairs of the building and listening for that strange laughter that is so often reported there.

IGNATIUS DONNELLY'S NININGER CITY HOME SITE

12899 Lock Boulevard, Hastings, Minnesota 55033

directions

From downtown St. Paul, take US-52 South for about 13.5 miles to Courthouse Boulevard. Stay on Courthouse Boulevard for about 5 miles and then turn left onto Mississippi Trail. Follow Mississippi Trail for a little more than 3.5 miles and then turn left onto Lock Boulevard. On your left, you should see a historic marker for the Ignatius Donnelly Home. The home itself is long gone, just a sparsely forested field and farmland remains.

history

Today Nininger is a ghost town, but in its day, it was one of the largest cities in the Minnesota Territory. The city was founded in the 1850s by John Nininger, brother-in-law of the governor of the territory, and Ignatius Donnelly. Hopes were high for the town. They hoped that the town would become the state capitol, but fate would spoil these plans. The Panic of 1857 essentially bankrupted the town, and when the railroads bypassed the town a couple of years later, the fate of Nininger was essentially sealed.

    Over the next few decades, the population of the town quickly diminished. Eventually, the entirety of the town was abandoned. Ignatius Donnelly, one of the founders of the town and one of the most famous people in Minnesota, was one of the last people to live there. Donnelly had been Lieutenant Governor of Minnesota and a congressman from Minnesota, but his real claim to fame came from the strange books he published. He published a book and gave lectures suggesting that Shakespeare's works were actually written by Francis Bacon. His most famous book was about the lost continent of Atlantis. He wrote that Atlantis was a real place in the middle of the Atlantic Ocean that was destroyed historically as Plato had suggested. He suggested that all world civilizations were derived from the original civilization in Atlantis.

Like Atlantis, Nininger is no more. It is a ghost town along a bend in the Mississippi River. In the 1930s, 30 years after Donnelly died and left his home abandoned, people were split as to whether the area should be converted to farmland or if the house should be saved and preserved as an historic site. The farmland advocates won, and the house was torn down. Today, all that remains is a small park and a plaque that tells of what once stood there.

ghost story

For Nininger, the moniker "ghost town" doesn't just mean it has been abandoned. According to some people, real ghosts roam the area that was once a bustling town of 1,000 people. Nowhere are these ghosts seen and heard more often than at the site where the town's most famous resident lived.

The most often reported story in the little grove that once held Donnelly's home is that strange, ghostly lights float around amongst the trees. Some report that these balls of light look like 19th-century lanterns roaming around, but other reports say they look more like floating balls of energy. Sometimes, these balls of light manifest in different colors, such as orange or red. No source is ever discovered for these mysterious lights. Other people in the area report a presence whether they are there during the day or the night. They feel as if they are being watched or followed throughout the area. Sometimes, people even hear footsteps behind them and will turn around to find no one there.

visiting

Today this area is just a little hill overlooking the Mississippi River. Officially, the little corner at Lock and 134th Street East is a little park remembering the town that was once here. There are no signs suggesting that the park closes at dark, so as long as you do not enter the adjacent farmland, you should be okay legally entering the small grove at dark. Park along the street and watch for those mysterious lights that float through the area, one last twinkle of the energy that was once here.

JESSIE TOMME SALON

92 Mahtomedi Avenue, Mahtomedi, Minnesota 55115

directions

From downtown Minneapolis, take I-35W North for almost 4 miles until you reach MN-36 East. Follow MN-36 East for 10 miles and then turn left onto Century Avenue North. Follow Century Avenue for two miles and then turn right onto Wildwood Road. Follow Wildwood Road for about a mile and a half and then continue straight onto Mahtomedi Avenue. Jessie Tomme Salon will be on your right.

history

Jessie Tomme Salon was founded by Jessie Tomme in 2005 and has operated as a high-end salon and spa since that time. It is considered one of the best, if not the best, salons in Minnesota; many people have come here and have been very impressed with the quality of the service.

The salon employs a spiritual healer who makes a living from the paranormal field. Perhaps her energy has left a mark upon the relatively recently constructed building.

ghost story

Despite the short and tragedy-free history of the Jessie Tomme Salon building, strange things happen here. Most of the paranormal activity seems to happen in the Purple Room on the second floor, where the spiritual healer works. Electromagnetic field detectors that have been used in this room have encountered high levels of electricity in the air. Further investigation shows no reason these fields should be here. Paranormal investigators usually believe there is a spike in these electric fields when a ghost is present.

These abnormal levels of energy are not the only thing to occur within the Purple Room. People feel as if someone else is in the room with them even when they are alone. Other times, people feel a breath on the back of their neck even though there is no one behind them. The curtains in front of the closet move by themselves when there is no draft in the room.

Throughout the rest of the building, people have seen strange shadows lurking about, which often appear as the sun is beginning to set, and the light is coming through the windows most prevalently.

visiting

To visit this haunted location, you will most likely need to enter during regular business hours and purchase one of their many services. Monday, the salon is open from 10 a.m.–8 p.m. Tuesday it is open from 10 a.m.–8:30 p.m. Wednesday and Thursday, it is open from 9:30 a.m.–8:30 p.m. The hours are more limited on the weekends. It is open from 9 a.m.–5 p.m. on Friday and from 9 a.m.–4 p.m. on Saturday. It is closed on Sunday. While many of the services involve beauty and relaxation, a psychic on staff does energy healing and card readings. The healing session takes 90 minutes and is $72; the card readings are $56. Those who work at the salon are aware and accepting of their ghosts and have allowed a paranormal investigation group into the salon to investigate the paranormal activity.

LEDUC MANSION

1629 Vermillion Street, Hastings, Minnesota 55033

directions

Take Warner Road from downtown St. Paul towards US-10 East. After almost 3 miles, Warner Road will end. Turn right to take US-10 East. US-10 will eventually become US-61 South, but you will continue to follow the road for almost 19 miles. After about 19 miles, the road heading north on the other side of the split highway will be called Vermillion Street. Since the mansion will be on your left between 16th and 17th Streets, you'll have to make a U-turn at 17th Street onto Vermillion Street in order to get to the mansion.

history

The history of this house started out innocently enough. A Civil War general named William Gates LeDuc decided to build as grand a house as he could on the somewhat modest budget he had. He succeeded, building a large home that he was proud to call his own.

Throughout the years after the Civil War, nothing really exceptional happened in the house. Servants would come and go, and the family lived happily off their land and in their grand estate. This sense of normality in the household ended around 1900. Around this time, General LeDuc's unmarried adult daughters became increasingly interested in Spiritualism. Around the time when their interest was peaking, their mother, the general's wife, passed away in the house.

At this point the General himself became interested in Spiritualism, and many séances were held within the house. Eventually, in 1917, the general himself passed away. His daughters ran the estate for a couple more decades but eventually were forced to sell the house. It became an antique shop and continued to operate as the shop until 1986 when the owner died, bequeathing the estate to the Minneapolis Historical Society.

Although the historical society wanted to turn it into a museum originally, it didn't have the funding to get the house up to specs. It sat abandoned for 20 years.

ghost story

As early as the 1950s, the house had the reputation of being haunted. In fact, Carroll Simmons, the owner of the antique store there, did his best to keep the atmosphere dark and creepy to encourage rumors of the building being haunted. The entities that haunted the house in the 1950s were reputed to be General LeDuc himself and his daughter Alice. Figures resembling these two people were seen in the dark recesses of the house. They often roamed aimlessly and then mysteriously disappeared.

In 1986, after Carroll Simmons died, and the house stood abandoned for 20 years, when people entered the house again, a new entity seemed to have joined the general and his daughter. Mr. Simmons is seen from time to time walking through the house as well.

Besides actually seeing apparitions in the building, other strange things happen. Doors suddenly slam shut for no reason. People hear footsteps when no one is there, and people feel intense cold spots in random areas throughout the house.

visiting

The activity at LeDuc Mansion happens exclusively inside the building. Luckily, the building is open as a museum to the public, and it is possible for tourists to enter the haunted place and perhaps encounter one of the resident ghosts.

From the end of May through the end of October, the house is open to the public on Wednesdays through Sundays until 5 p.m. There are tours every hour and a half with the first one starting at 10 a.m. every day except Sunday when the first tour is at 1 p.m.

MILL HOUSE GALLERY

516 North Pine Street, Chaska, Minnesota 55318

directions

From downtown Minneapolis, take I-35W South for about 4 miles to exit 11, MN-62 West. Follow MN-62 for another 5.5 miles until you reach US-212 West. Follow US-212 for a little more than 12 miles until you reach the Chestnut Street exit. Turn left onto North Chestnut Street and follow that road for about 2 miles. Turn right onto West Sixth Street and then take the first left onto North Pine Street. The Mill House Gallery will be on your left.

history

The building that is today the Mill House Gallery was originally a house where a man named William Scott lived. William Scott owned an important flour mill in the area and became wealthy from the proceeds from that mill. As his wealth grew, he became more and more involved with the community, donating both his time and his money to many local causes, including a local baseball team that bears his flour brand name, the White Diamonds.

At the height of his wealth and popularity within the community, in 1933, William Scott died. At the time of his death there were no reports that he was depressed or that anyone had any personal problems with the man. The cause of his death, though, was officially listed as death by cyanide. At the time of his death, many assumed he'd died as a result of suicide, but due to the fact that he wasn't depressed and had no enemies, it is also possible that his death was the result of an accidental poisoning.

ghost story

Perhaps William Scott continues to roam his old house, trying to let people know that he hadn't killed himself but had instead died as a result of an accident. Shadows are often seen roaming throughout the house without any apparent source. A shadow passes in front of a doorway, and the witness will investigate to see who is there but will find no one. Shadows tend to manifest throughout the building, and even lights from passing cars outside cannot account for their frequency or appearance.

Other times, strange sounds occur throughout the house. Footsteps and creaking are the most frequent. Again, these sounds have no apparent source even after extensive investigation. Another strange occurrence involved several ornaments that were hanging from strings within the gallery. For no reason, three of the ornaments began swinging violently back and forth. The ornaments were not hanging next to one another and then, instead of slowing to a stop, the ornaments just suddenly stopped swinging.

visiting

Today, the Mill House Gallery is an art studio and a gift shop with regular hours. To visit the ghosts here, you will need to enter the building during regular business hours, which are always subject to change. As of the time this book was written, the building is open Thursday through Saturday from 10 a.m.–6 p.m. It is closed from November 1 until January.

MINNEAPOLIS INSTITUTE OF THE ARTS

2400 Third Avenue South, Minneapolis, Minnesota 55404

directions

From the river in downtown Minneapolis, take Third Avenue South for about a mile and a half until you reach East 24th Street. The art museum will be on your right. It is a large structure, which encompasses an entire city block. There is parking along the streets that surround the museum. The front entrance is on East 24th Street across from the park.

history

This museum was built in 1915 to house the growing collection of the Minneapolis Society of Fine Arts, which until that time had displayed their art collection in various locations around the city, including the Minneapolis Public Library. The society was founded in 1883 by the wealthy sector of the city with the intention of bringing an understanding and appreciation of fine art to the city. The original part of the structure built in 1915 was designed by one of the most renowned architectural firms in the state and depended heavily upon turn-of-the-century French architectural influences.

Throughout the years since the original building was constructed, several other sections and wings have been added by equally renowned architects, making this building one of the most impressive in the entire city. Throughout the many years the Minneapolis Institute of the Arts has existed, many important and beautiful works of art have passed through its doors. Perhaps some remnants of the artists have remained within the building itself.

ghost story

Compared to many of the places in this book, the ghosts here seem to be quite tame. This being said, there is a tangible sense that something paranormal exists within these walls. Perhaps the ghosts are remnants of the artists who put their heart and soul into their works displayed here. Perhaps the ghosts are admirers of art, come back to eternally wander through these hallowed hallways.

The ghostly happening that occurs most frequently within this museum is people experiencing cold spots. In some strange location within the museum where there shouldn't be any breeze and where there isn't any air conditioning vent, people suddenly feel incredibly cold. According to modern paranormal thought, unexplainable cold spots can be an indication that a ghost has manifested itself in the immediate area.

Beyond these cold spots, people often hear footsteps in the same room they are standing in, even when they are alone and not walking around. These cold spots and footsteps happen most often in the Connecticut Room. Paranormal groups have made audio recordings within the building as well and have heard strange voices on their recordings that they didn't hear at the time the recording was made.

visiting

To visit the ghosts here, you need to enter the building during regular business hours. It is open from 10 a.m.–5 p.m. on Tuesday, Wednesday, Friday, and Saturday. On Thursday, it is open from 10 a.m.–9 p.m., and on Sunday it is open from 11 a.m.–5 p.m. The museum is closed on Mondays.

You are able to make audio recordings and take photographs for personal or educational use. Most of the activity seems concentrated in the Connecticut Room and on the third floor of the building.

MINNESOTA STATE PUBLIC SCHOOL ORPHANAGE MUSEUM

540 West Hills Circle, Owatonna, Minnesota 55060

directions

From downtown St. Paul, take I-35E South for 45 miles to exit 42A, the Owatonna exit. Merge onto Hoffman Drive Northwest and then turn right onto State Avenue. Take another right onto West Hills Circle. The orphanage museum will be on your left.

history

The orphanage was built in 1885. It was originally called the State Public School for Dependent and Neglected Children. Many children in the area were left orphaned, and they were in danger of either freezing to death during the harsh Minnesota winters or starving to death in the face of their neglect. Minnesota Legislature passed an act chartering this school and orphanage so that these children would have a chance to live. The site was chosen because it was along major rail lines and near the more densely populated rural sections of the state.

Although there were many children who wouldn't have otherwise had a chance at life who were able to live out happy lives because of this place, many other children did not make it through. More than 10,000 children passed through this building, either eventually moving on or passing away from any number of things while they were housed here. A cemetery on the grounds holds the bodies of several hundred of these children. Some were beaten to death with a radiator brush in a third-floor room called the "tower room," which was used for disciplining children; some simply died of disease or killed themselves. The grounds are infested with the spirits of those children who did not have a chance at life.

By 1945, the orphanage was no more. Until 1970, the grounds operated as a school for mentally disabled people. In 1970, the grounds were completely abandoned for four years before the city set up administrative offices there. In 1992, they began to restore much of the original orphanage to set up the museum currently housed on the grounds.

ghost story

Throughout the entirety of the old orphanage grounds, people report all kinds of strange things. Most of the time, people are assaulted by intangible feelings of discomfort or cold chills on hot days. They are unable to explain exactly how they are feeling, just that they do not feel welcome or that they feel as if they are being watched by some unseen presence. But there are more tangible instances of hauntings.

An elevator in the main building sometimes goes to the floor where someone is waiting and opens its doors despite the fact that no one has touched a button. Throughout the grounds, people see figures dressed in period clothing, but the figures mysteriously vanish when approached. People hear children giggling when there are no children nearby and hear balls rolling across the floor when there is nothing there.

Many local law enforcement officers believe the place is haunted. Regularly, they receive 911 calls from a basement room in the main building at the orphanage. When they respond, not only is there no one there, but the room itself is locked.

visiting

The only time that it is possible to visit this haunted location in hopes of experiencing some of the ghostly activity here would be during their regular business hours. The building is open until 5 p.m. every day of the week. It opens at 8 a.m. on Monday through Friday, and at 1 p.m. on Saturday and Sunday.

While some of the haunted areas, such as the tower and the basement room where the 911 calls come from, are closed to the public, many of the other haunted places are open to explore on your own. You can walk through the children's graveyard on the grounds and explore the main building where many of the strange sounds and occurrences have been known to happen.

PADELFORD PACKETBOAT COMPANY

205 Doctor Justus Ohage Boulevard, St. Paul,
Minnesota 55107

directions

From St. Paul, take Wabasha Street to the south over the Mississippi River. Follow
this road for about a half mile until you reach Plato Boulevard. Turn right onto Plato
Boulevard West. Follow Plato for a half mile until it dead-ends into Dr. Justus Ohage
Boulevard. Turn right onto Dr. Justus Ohage Boulevard. This will take you directly
into the Padelford Packet Boat Company.

history

The Padelford Packet Boat Company was founded in 1969 and has run continuously
since then. They offer chartered boat rides on the Mississippi River and public tours
of the river on actual steamboats. The history of the place may seem short and
uneventful, but a tragic event happened on one of their boats, which may have created
the ghost that haunts this place.

A man was out on the Jonathan Padelford steamboat in the Mississippi River
when he decided to go for a swim. He started to climb to the roof of the pilothouse

so he could dive into the river. Unfortunately, as he was almost up to the roof of the pilothouse, he slipped and fell towards the river below. On his way down he hit his back on the guardrail before falling into the river. The collision with the guardrail paralyzed him, and he drowned in the river, unable to swim to safety.

ghost story

The ghost on the Jonathan Padelford seems to constantly replay the events that occurred on that fateful day when the man drowned after hitting the guardrail. Passengers and crewmen on the ship sometimes hear the sounds of footsteps climbing the stairs to the top of the pilothouse. Soon after the footsteps stop at the top of the pilothouse, a large splash is heard in the water adjacent to the boat. When these sounds are investigated, no one is ever able to find any explanation. No one has climbed the stairs, and there is nothing in the water but the ship.

visiting

Many different events and cruises are offered to the public on the Jonathan Padelford. Going on one of these cruises would be your only opportunity to ride on the vessel and to maybe hear the ghost that supposedly haunts the pilothouse.

Sightseeing cruises are offered every Saturday and Sunday during the summer. These cruises start at 2 p.m. and display such sights as caves, bridges, and the mouth of the Minnesota River. The sightseeing cruises last about an hour and a half and are your best bet as a tourist to take a leisurely cruise on a haunted steamship. Other cruises offer dinner or other special events, but are subject to change. You can check out their Web site to get a schedule of these events.

PARTY PAPERS

222 East Main Street, Anoka, Minnesota 55303

directions

Take I-94 North from downtown Minneapolis for about 4.5 miles to MN-252 North. Follow MN-252 for another 4 miles and then merge onto MN-610 West. Follow MN-610 for about 4.5 more miles and then merge onto US-169 North. Follow US-169 for 5 miles and then turn right onto Main Street. Party Papers is on your right.

history

The building that currently houses Party Papers doesn't have a direct connection with any tragic occurrences, but it is located in a historic building in the older Main Street district of Anoka. Many shops and stores have occupied this building since its creation, and perhaps some remnant of those who worked or shopped at those establishments has stayed behind.

Anoka itself proudly displays a rather creepy moniker come October. It bills itself as the Halloween Capitol of the World due to a Halloween festival and parade that has been held almost every year since 1920. Perhaps this celebration of the paranormal and macabre has invited some spirits to live here in the heart of the Halloween universe.

ghost story

A psychic once told the store owner that a short, balding man with white sleeves was haunting the front of the store. The psychic said he was the owner of a shop that used to be on the property. While no one has reported actually seeing the apparition of this man, the "Open" sign on the front window sometimes goes on and off for no reason, at all times of the day and night.

People, including the owner of the store, have spotted an apparition standing in the back of the store. Witnesses see the figure out of the corner of their eye, but when they look again, they find absolutely no one is there. In the back of the store, items mysteriously fall off the shelves when there is no one nearby. This has even happened during the night when there was no one at all in the building. Other times, people are touched or pushed by unseen forces while walking through the store.

visiting

The front of the Party Papers building contains large windows. If you want to try to see an apparition at the back of the store, you can look through those windows late at night long after the building has closed. The best way to find ghosts here, though, is to enter during regular business hours. Sunday, it's open from 11 a.m.–4 p.m. Monday, it's open from 10:30 a.m.–7 p.m. Tuesday through Thursday, it's open from 10 a.m.–8 p.m. Friday, it's open 10 a.m.–7 p.m., and Saturday from 9:30 a.m.–6p.m.

SCHMITT MUSIC

2400 Freeway Boulevard, Brooklyn Center, Minnesota 55430

directions

Take I-94 West from downtown Minneapolis for about 5.5 miles to exit 34, the Shingle Creek Parkway exit. Take the ramp to Shingle Creek Parkway North and then turn left onto Shingle Creek Parkway. Take the first left onto Freeway Boulevard, and Schmitt Music will be on your right.

history

Schmitt Music Company was founded in 1896 by Paul Schmitt, who had previously managed Century Piano's sheet music department. Due to differences with Century Piano, Schmitt started his own music business, which originally opened on Tenth Street in Minneapolis. Throughout the years, the business has expanded to the Twin Cities suburbs and to many surrounding states. The warehouse for the company was moved to the Brooklyn Center location.

According to legend, several years ago an employee suffered a heart attack in the doorway leading to the warehouse and died as a result. According to the store's management, though, this never occurred. No one has ever committed suicide within the building. That being said, a man was found dead by a picnic area near the woods behind the store. All the employees of Schmitt Music Company are expert musicians. The man who reportedly had the heart attach was an expert pianist but knew how to play other instruments as well.

ghost story

According to rumors and legends, the man who supposedly died in the doorway haunts the building to this day. Most of the time, the paranormal happenings occur after the store has closed for the evening.

Employees who are cleaning up after the patrons have left for the day report hearing strange things. The sound most reported is a piano playing. Employees have heard a piano playing somewhere in the store or in the warehouse, even though no one is actually playing the pianos. These employees often make an exhaustive search to find who is playing the piano but are unable to find anyone. Sometimes, it isn't just the pianos that play by themselves—employees hear horns, guitars, and even drums play by themselves after all the customers have left for the night. Perhaps the man who died here is doing his best to compose a paranormal musical masterpiece after his unfortunate passing.

visiting

Unfortunately, to really experience the ghost at Schmitt Music, you almost have to be an employee because the mysterious music that plays often plays after the store has closed for the night. The store is alive with the sounds of many different instruments being tested by customers throughout the day. Perhaps the actual music playing during business hours dampens the paranormal music that plays in the background. Your best chance as a nonemployee to experience the ghosts here is to go when it is not busy and rather quiet. Then, if you hear a distant piano playing, perhaps you're hearing music from beyond the grave.

SKATIN' PLACE

3302 Southway Drive, Saint Cloud, Minnesota 56301

directions

From downtown Minneapolis, take I-94 West for 58 miles to exit 171, the CR-7 North exit. Follow CR-7 North for another 2 miles and then turn left onto 33rd Street S. Turn left onto Southway Drive. Skatin' Place will be on your left.

history

Until the 1970s, the land that this building currently occupies was nothing more than swampland, which was actually rather dangerous. Children exploring the area could get stuck in the mud or fall into an unexpectedly deep section of the swamp, so locals warned their children to stay away from the area. One particular story circulates about a young child named Gilbert who lived in the area in the early 1900s. Despite his parents' repeated warnings to stay away from the swamp, Gilbert was found dead face down in the water one day.

In the 1970s, the swampland was drained and the skating rink was built. Apparently, though, not all traces of the area's history were destroyed.

ghost story

Those who know about the ghost at the Skatin' Place skating rink have named him Gilbert. Perhaps they assume the ghost is a remnant of the child who passed away here so many years ago. The paranormal activity here does have a somewhat childish and prankish feel to it, adding to the assumption that the ghost is the spirit of poor Gilbert.

Most of the ghostly activity here has to do with electronics or plumbing. The lights in the building sometimes flicker on and off by themselves for no reason. Music equipment malfunctions for no reason. Faucets in the bathrooms turn on and off by themselves, and toilets flush by themselves. No one has ever actually seen an apparition of little Gilbert, but some people know that he is constantly around, messing with things.

visiting

In order to visit the ghosts here, you need to enter during regular business hours. These business hours are subject to change and can get rather complicated. On Tuesdays from 4–7 p.m., the building is open for anyone to skate. Renting skates costs $1.50 and admission costs $5. From 7–9 p.m. on Tuesdays, the rink is open to adults only for the same price. On Wednesdays and Thursdays, the building is available to rent out for private parties. Fridays, it is open from 6–9:30 p.m. with a $13 admission fee (all inclusive), and on Saturday and Sunday it is open until 5 p.m. for a cost of $5.50.

THE SOAP FACTORY

518 Second Street SE, Minneapolis, Minnesota 55414

directions

Take Second Street from the heart of downtown Minneapolis. The Soap Factory is just a block away from the Mississippi River. It is at the corner of Second Street SE and Fifth Avenue SE, and it is near Hennepin Island Park and the Stone Arch Bridge. The building is actually an old soap factory, and its exterior still appears as such.

history

Although today the building houses a contemporary art gallery, the building itself looks old because it actually is old—built in 1892 as a railroad warehouse. At that time, the building was only one story tall. Throughout the years, the building changed hands and was used for a variety of things. The factory building produced batteries and syrup throughout many of its early years before eventually becoming a soap factory in 1924, run by the National Purity Soap Company.

By 1992, the company that ran the factory moved to another part of Minnesota, leaving the giant building completely empty in the heart of the city's warehouse district. For three years it sat vacant until a contemporary art group called No Name Exhibitions showed interest in purchasing the building. Willing to donate to the cause and unwilling to spend money to refurbish or repair the old dilapidated building, the Pillsbury Company, which then owned the building, sold it to No Name Exhibitions for $1, leaving to the artists the responsibility of repairing the massive building. Today the three-story building is a working art gallery. The top floor contains studio space, while the first floor is an expansive gallery space. The basement is a confusing maze, which is used only once a year for a haunted house.

ghost story

While, specifically, there are no actual documented tragedies that may have caused the ghostly activity here, the age of the building and its history could likely cause the paranormal phenomena. The most commonly reported activity is footsteps. When the footsteps are investigated, there is no one there. The most common place where the footsteps are heard is on a wooden staircase leading from the gallery floor to the basement.

Footsteps are not the only unusual activity in this building, though. People often hear voices when there is no one there talking. Witnesses are startled by short breaths in their ears or by distant screams. Other times, people clearly hear someone say, "Help me," although there is no one there.

Also, the building is apparently infested with shadow people. Throughout the building, people see shadows walking through corridors that simply vanish into thin air. Cameras have caught strange human shadows at times when there is no one there.

visiting

During most of the year, the gallery level of the Soap Factory is open Thursday through Sunday. On Thursday and Friday, the gallery is open from 2 p.m.–8 p.m., while on Saturday and Sunday, it is open from noon until 5 p.m. During most of the year, this would be your best chance to visit this historic and incredibly haunted building. Admission is free during these times, but they do accept donations at the door.

In October, though, you have a much better opportunity to get scared at the Soap Factory. They run a haunted house in the basement from October 1 through Halloween. It is $10 and tickets are only available at the door. It is a very creepy way to explore this haunted building.

WABASHA STREET CAVES

215 Wabasha Street South, St. Paul, Minnesota 55107

directions

From the St. Paul City Hall, just take Wabasha Street South across the river until you get to the intersection of Wabasha and Plato Boulevard. The caves will be on your right just past Plato Boulevard. There is a parking lot out front.

history

The caves aren't actually caves at all but are officially mines, since they were carved out by human hands. They were started in the 1870s to mine silica deposits in the sandstone but were then used to farm mushrooms as early as 1890. The more well-known history of the caves started during Prohibition in the 1920s.

According to many stories, St. Paul was a safe haven for gangsters who were on the run from the law. The stories went that as long as these wanted felons paid a bribe to the local police and they didn't commit any crimes in the city limits, they were safe from prosecution and extradition. The Wabasha Street Caves housed a popular speakeasy that is said to have hosted such famous mobsters as John Dillinger and Ma Barker during its life as an illegal liquor establishment.

More rumors circulate about an execution that occurred in one of the back rooms of the caves. Three gangsters were supposedly executed there in the 1920s and then interred underneath the concrete floors.

ghost story

These tunnels are infested with spirits. Most of the ghosts that inhabit these tunnels are actually full-figure apparitions. People often encounter men who are dressed in 1920s suits walking through the tunnels. While at first the witnesses always assume these figures are costumed guides from the staff at the caves, sometimes these figures walk through walls or simply disappear without a trace. There is also the apparition of a woman who appears in period clothing. Those who have seen her assume she is a madam, Nina Clifford, who once worked in the caves.

Besides the apparitions that are often sighted within the tunnels, people see strange fogs that appear and dissipate without rhyme or reason. Once a small child told his mother that he had fun playing with the gangsters at the wedding they had attended at the caves. The child insisted that the gangsters weren't employees in costume, and photographs of the child at the wedding showed him surrounded by a strange fog. A bartender also haunts the bar at the Wabasha Street Caves. Sometimes when people finish drinking a glass of wine at the bar, they turn around to find the glass has been refilled, but no one was there to refill it.

visiting

There are several ways to visit the caves. Every Thursday night at 7:00, the caves host "Swing Night," where music and dancing go on throughout the night. There are also tours that go through the caves. Historic tours of the caves are on Thursday nights at 5:00, and Saturday or Sunday mornings at 11:00. Ghost tours go through the caves during October. These ghost tours may be your best chance to encounter the ghosts and hear all the stories from the people who have experienced them. The schedule for these ghost tours is always subject to change. To get the current times, check the Web site at www.wabashastreetcaves.com.

There are other entrances to the caves throughout the area, which have warnings posted and barricades set up so that you do not enter through these entrances. This is for your own safety. Within the last few years, at least five teenagers have died while breaking into the caves. Due to poor ventilation, these alternative closed entrances create buildups of carbon monoxide, a poisonous gas. Stick to the tours, and don't break in under any circumstances.

WARDEN'S HOUSE MUSEUM
602 North Main Street, Stillwater, Minnesota 55082

directions
Take I-35E North from St. Paul for almost 4 miles to exit 111A, MN-36 East towards Stillwater. After about 16.5 miles, the road changes its name to South Main Street/MN-95. Just past East Mulberry Street, the Warden's House Museum will be on your left. Parking is available across from the museum on Main Street.

history
This house was the home of the warden of the Minnesota Territorial Prison as early as 1853, which was when it was built. Throughout the years that it served as a home for the warden, 13 different wardens called the building home. The ghost at the house involves the last warden to live here, Henry Wolfer, who resided at the house until 1914.

When Warden Wolfer lived in the house, his daughter Gertrude became pregnant and gave birth to a boy. Tragically, soon after the birth of her son, Gertrude died of acute appendicitis. The baby was sent to live with his grandparents at the warden's house until they moved out of the house in 1914.

Since 1941, the house has operated as a museum. Many tourists go through the house during its months of operation.

ghost story

According to many witnesses, the ghost of Gertrude still haunts the old warden's house. Those who are aware of her existence suggest that when she died suddenly, she followed her son to the warden's house, but when her father moved out in 1914, Gertrude stayed.

Gertrude manifests herself in a couple of different ways. The first way involves a cradle that is displayed in one of the upstairs bedrooms of the museum. From time to time, the cradle mysteriously begins to rock back and forth. There is no breeze blowing in the house and no reason the cradle would suddenly begin to rock back and forth.

Others will actually see an apparition of Gertrude herself roaming the halls of the museum. These witnesses encounter a ghostly woman walking from room to room. She appears to be looking for something; perhaps after all these years she is still looking for her baby. Other witnesses see Gertrude looking out towards Main Street from one of the upstairs windows.

visiting

The museum has rather limited hours—from 1 to 5 p.m. from Thursday through Sunday; it is only open from May until September. These are the only times you can enter the house in an attempt to see Gertrude roaming the building or to see the cradle rock back and forth by itself.

However, this isn't the only time you can see the ghost here, though. Gertrude is also seen looking out from an upstairs window. If you go to the house when it is not open, you still may be able to see Gertrude watching the road from one of the upstairs windows.

SECTION IV

food, spirits, and lodging

BILLY'S BAR & GRILL

214 Jackson Street, Anoka, Minnesota 55303

directions

From downtown Minneapolis, take I-94 West for about 4.5 miles to the MN-252 North exit. Follow MN-252 North for about 4 miles and then exit onto MN-610 West on the left side of the highway. Follow MN-610 West for about 4.5 miles to US-169 North and follow that for a little more than 5 miles. Turn right onto East Main Street and then left onto North Second Avenue. Take the first right onto Jackson Street, and Billy's Bar & Grill will be on your right.

history

Due to some of the immoral things that the building was reputedly used for and to the public's view of suicide at the beginning of the 20th century, it is hard to determine exactly what transpired in this building during its years of existence. We do know for sure that the original building was built as the Anoka Hotel in 1877 by a man named Charles Jackson, who lived there during its early years with his wife, Lotta. We know that during the Great Anoka Fire of 1884, the building was severely damaged. We know that the very next year, 1885, Anoka's first murder occurred in the street just outside of the hotel. A couple of friends were talking in the street when suddenly one of them took out a pistol and started shooting. The other man, Peter Gross, suddenly became aware that his friend was actually shooting at him. As he began to flee, he took a bullet in the back. He was able to crawl inside the hotel where he was taken to one of the upper floors to die.

Many other stories about the hotel may or may not be true. One story, which is probably true, was that the building was used as a brothel during the late 1800s and early 1900s. During one unfortunate business transaction with a prominent client, one of the prostitutes (supposedly sporting beautiful red hair) was killed. Her body was smuggled from the hotel and never found.

Another story, which may or may not be true, involved Jackson's wife, Lotta. Official records of the time list that Lotta (a red-haired woman herself) died of pneumonia at a nearby cottage in 1918. Most people who know of Lotta, though, suggest that her death was a much darker affair. Many people believe Lotta hung herself on the third floor of the hotel in full sight of the window and the street below, and she was discovered by passersby in the street.

ghost story

While the most verifiable piece of tragic history in this building involves the shooting of Peter Gross, the phantoms who haunt this place seem to be someone different. The ghost seen here most often is reported to be a woman with red hair. She is seen in a couple of different places in a couple of different ways. Sometimes, the apparition is spotted from outside of the building. Passersby look up to the third floor during all hours of the day or night and see a woman with red hair looking out to the street below. Other times, people inside the restaurant see a woman with red hair walk through the restaurant and then mysteriously vanish.

Other times, things in the building move by themselves and strange noises are reported. People hear voices, doors closing, and footsteps coming from places they are certain are empty. Pictures displayed on the walls tilt back and forth for no reason, and glasses and silverware move across the table by themselves.

visiting

There are a couple of ways to experience the ghosts at Billy's. The easiest way is to pass the building at any time during the day or night and look up to the third-floor windows to try to spot the apparition of the red-haired lady. To experience the apparition in the restaurant or the strange sounds or moving objects, you need to enter the establishment during regular business hours. It opens at 9 a.m. every day of the week and is open until 1 a.m. Monday through Thursday; until 2 a.m. on Friday and Saturday; and until midnight on Sundays.

THE BUSTED NUT

118 Second Street East, Hastings, Minnesota 55033

directions

Take US-61 South from downtown St. Paul for about 18 miles until you reach
Hastings, Minnesota. Turn right when you get to West Third Street and then take the
first right onto The Great River Road. When The Great River Road dead-ends into
West Second Street, turn right. The Busted Nut will be on your right in the heart of
the downtown area.

history

There are a couple of different versions of the history that may have created the ghost
haunting this place. The first story is less verifiable than the second. The first story
goes that, while the building was being used as another restaurant, the owner of that
restaurant killed himself in the back kitchen area of the building. This story is likely
more legend than fact, since we couldn't locate anything to verify this story.

Another story about the origins of this ghost, though, is quite a bit more verifiable.
A couple of men were sitting on the roof of the building when it was still being used as

a restaurant called Treat Me Sweet. They had been drinking while up there, and one of the men slipped and fell off the roof to his death.

ghost story

Most of the ghost stories here in the Busted Nut occur on the upper level of the building. People who go up there, especially when they are up there alone, feel very uncomfortable and unwelcome. Some employees refuse to even go to the upper level of the building, period. Besides these feelings of discomfort, people have heard footsteps coming from the upstairs when there is no one up there and seen shadows moving around in the upstairs.

Rarely do these feelings of unease spread to the downstairs of the building. Every once in a while something strange happens in the main area on the first floor, though. A chair moves slightly by itself. Something falls when there is no one near it. Most of the activity, though, is centered in the upstairs of the building.

visiting

The Busted Nut is open late into the evenings, so you can certainly enter the bar after dark. The atmosphere of the bar is sometimes quite loud, though, so it can be difficult at times to hear anything happening in the upstairs, which is off-limits to the public. Your best bet would probably be to enter the bar when it is most quiet and not very busy, which would usually be in the afternoons. Second-story windows are visible from the street, which means you can see into the haunted second floor from the street after the building closes.

DAIRY QUEEN

2612 Highway 88, St. Anthony, Minnesota 55418

directions

From downtown Minneapolis, take I-35W North for about a mile and a half to exit 21A, the New Brighton Boulevard exit. At the end of the ramp, turn left onto New Brighton Boulevard and follow that road for a little more than a mile. The Dairy Queen will be on your left across the street from Hillside Cemetery and Sunset Memorial Park.

history

Despite the vast variety of paranormal activities that occur from time to time at this Dairy Queen, not a lot of history here may have caused it. This Dairy Queen was built in 1988 and has been a Dairy Queen under the same management since the day it was built. There have been countless teenage employees who have worked here throughout the years, but there has never been a death inside the building.

While there hasn't really been anything tragic happen inside the Dairy Queen, it is directly across the street from a large cemetery. Perhaps some of the ghosts from the cemetery just really want some ice cream.

ghost story

Strange things often happen within this Dairy Queen. Much of the activity seems to center around the employees. When no customers are in the store, employees sometimes hear someone loudly call out their names. When they investigate, they find no one there had actually yelled anything. After the store is closed, employees sometimes hear what sound like little children laughing inside the store. Again, an investigation of the sounds turns up nothing.

While the store is open, all varieties of strange things happen. Food in the freezer falls off the shelves when there is no one in there. Receipts suddenly print out for orders that were never made. Trays that had been neatly stacked suddenly are placed on the tables in front of every chair.

visiting

While employees have experienced most of the activity at the Dairy Queen, it is still possible to experience some of the phenomena yourself, even if you don't work here. The fake receipts, the crashing sounds in the back, and possibly the laughter of the phantom children are all things to pay attention to while you're there. Of course, you can only enter the building while they're open, and the best time to run into a ghost while you're there is when it is not busy.

DOUBLETREE BY HILTON HOTEL

7800 Normandale Boulevard, Bloomington, Minnesota 55439

directions

From downtown Minneapolis, take I-394 West for about 3.5 miles until you get to exit 5, MN-100 South. Follow MN-100 South for about 8 miles until you reach the Industrial Boulevard exit. Go straight at the end of the exit. This will take you onto Normandale Boulevard. The Doubletree Hotel will be on your right.

history

This building was originally constructed as a hotel in the 1970s. It was known as the Radisson South and was near the Metropolitan Stadium, "The Met," where the Vikings and Twins played. Nothing exceptional really happened with the hotel until 1996, when it underwent intensive renovations to bring it into the modern age. It has since changed hands several times. It was a Sheraton Hotel for many years and has since changed once again to a Hilton Doubletree Hotel.

Throughout its many years as a hotel, many people have stayed here. Today, it is near the Mall of America, one of the most popular tourist attractions in the entire state. At least one suicide has occurred at the building. Someone leapt to their death from the roof.

ghost story

It is hard to say who haunts this building. This building has surely seen its share of excitement and tragedy. We were unable to uncover any instances of anyone actually seeing a ghost at the hotel. Most of the ghost stories involve sounds or feelings.

Often, people report feeling that a presence is approaching them. They are unable to explain the feeling any better than that. They are simply terrified, explaining that they are certain that something is coming at them.

Other witnesses often report sounds throughout the building. Most often, they hear footsteps approaching them down the hallways and inside the rooms. They are never able to find the source of the footsteps. Other people hear sobbing coming from their rooms or loud banging that people in the next room are unable to hear.

visiting

It would be frowned upon if you were to enter the hotel just to roam around looking for ghosts. You would likely be asked to leave. This is a business, though, and if you wanted to spend the night in a haunted hotel, the rooms are reasonably priced, and the paranormal activity has been reported within the rooms themselves. There is also a restaurant on the property you could go to if you weren't willing to spend the money for a night in the hotel.

FIRST AVENUE NIGHTCLUB

701 First Avenue North, Minneapolis, Minnesota 55403

directions

From the heart of downtown Minneapolis, simply, as its name suggests, take First Avenue towards Seventh Street. The nightclub is one of the most popular and bustling clubs in the city, so if you're driving down First Avenue and see a large group of people, you are likely in the right spot. The club is on the corner of First Avenue and Seventh Street. There are stars with names of bands and artists that have played here flanking the doors and a large sign out front.

history

The building can trace its origins back to the late 1930s when it was originally constructed as a Greyhound Bus station. Its original art deco design made it a favorite architectural fixture to many native Minnesotans. Eventually, the bus station was moved from the building, and several small stores inhabited the beautiful structure from time to time. It wasn't until 1970 that investors realized its potential as a dance club.

Since 1970, First Avenue has been the quintessential nightclub in Minnesota and has held live performances by many of the greatest musical artists of the 1970s, 1980s,

1990s, and today. During the time it was a dance club, there was only one truly dark and tragic incident that occurred, which could be the reason for the ghost here. A young blond woman hung herself in one of the stalls in the women's restroom.

ghost story

Several ghosts still haunt this iconic nightclub. The first involves the apparition of a young blond woman who is always seen wearing a green jacket. Those who see her don't always recognize her as a ghost at first. They only realize something is wrong when she suddenly vanishes before their eyes. Once, the blond girl with the green jacket was seen in a stall in the women's restroom with a noose around her neck. She was seen in the fifth stall.

While the woman in the green jacket is the most famous ghost at the nightclub, other strange things happen from time to time. Apparently, the ghosts like to join the living on the dance floor. When the strobes are flashing and large groups of people are dancing, some observant people realize that some of the dancers have no legs but are instead floating above the floor. Other times, DJs at the club hear strange voices and creepy sounds come through their headphones as they are listening to the music.

visiting

In order to experience any of the ghosts at the club, you have to go when the club is open for business. The events being presented and the prices for those events are all subject to change. The club's Web site offers a calendar of events listing prices and dates the club is open. Your best chance to encounter the ghosts here is to go during an especially crowded dance night. Look for a blond in a green jacket and make sure that if you're dancing with someone on the dance floor, your partner has legs.

FITZGERALD THEATER

10 East Exchange Street, St. Paul, Minnesota 55101

directions

Take Wabasha Street north from the river in downtown St. Paul and turn right onto Exchange Street East. The Theater will be near the corner and will be on your right.

history

Built in 1910, the Fitzgerald Theater is the oldest standing theater in St. Paul. Throughout its long history, it has presented many different types of shows and performances. It started out showing stage plays and soon moved into the vaudeville scene. By 1933, the theater was showing movies, which it continued to do for some time. Throughout its history, the theater has had many names. It wasn't until 1994 that the building's name was finally changed to the Fitzgerald Theater, after acclaimed St. Paul native F. Scott Fitzgerald. Today, the theater hosts one of the most popular public radio programs in the country, "A Prairie Home Companion," and was the setting for the 2005 movie of the same name.

While many things have occurred in this theater throughout its years of existence, most people trace its paranormal history back to a single incident. While many of the details of the incident are fuzzy at best, essentially what happened is that a stagehand named Ben was somehow killed while working in the theater. He was known to his peers as unreliable and as a prankster.

ghost story

Strange things happen in this theater. People hear what sounds like beer bottles clinking together backstage. When they investigate the sounds, there are no bottles or people back there. The catwalks above the stage also play host to some strange shadows. People see the shadow of a man walking around on the catwalks. No sound accompanies this shadow, and when people investigate further, they find no one is ever actually up there. Sometimes, the figure on the catwalks becomes somewhat dangerous. Items seem to be tossed from the catwalk down onto the stage. Once, a large piece of plaster narrowly missed several workers who were working on the stage.

An entrance to the theater has long been closed off, but despite the fact that the entrance is now closed, people standing near it still sometimes feel a cold breeze flow past them, as if someone had just opened the door and allowed the cold air to flow in.

visiting

The events and shows at the Fitzgerald change from week to week. You need to go to the theater's Web site at www.fitzgeraldtheater.publicradio.org or call them at (651) 290-1200 to find out the showtimes and prices. To enter the theater, you need to purchase tickets to one of their shows. Since the ghost of Ben is seen and heard exclusively inside of the theater, purchasing tickets is the only way to catch a glimpse of this ghost.

FOREPAUGH'S RESTAURANT

276 South Exchange Street, St. Paul, Minnesota 55102

directions

Take the bridge at Wabasha Street in St. Paul over the river and then turn left onto Kellogg. Follow Kellogg until you reach the intersection with Exchange Street just past the Science Center parking lot. Turn left and follow Exchange Street for three blocks. Forepaugh's will be on your left. It overlooks Irvine Park.

history

While today this building is a successful restaurant in the heart of St. Paul, originally, this building was a mansion built by a successful dry goods wholesaler, Joseph Forepaugh, for his wife and his daughters. After building the impressive mansion, Forepaugh decided he had more disposable income, so to create more of a life of excess, he hired several servants to work in the house for him.

Things went well until Joseph Forepaugh fell in love with one of the servant girls named Molly. A torrid love affair progressed and continued until, one day, Joseph's wife walked in on them as they were making love. Furious, she insisted that he never see the servant again and that he fire her. By this time, though, Molly was pregnant and couldn't deal with the thought of never seeing her child's father again. She went to the third floor of the house and tied a noose to a light fixture near the Exchange Street window. She threw herself out of the window with the noose around her neck to end her life.

Joseph was completely crushed by this and eventually couldn't handle it any longer himself. He took one of his pistols to nearby train tracks and shot himself as an oncoming train bore down upon him.

ghost story

The ghosts of both Molly and Joseph are said to haunt this house to this day. They have learned a lesson from their mistakes of the past, though, and are never actually seen together within the house. Perhaps they wait until the building is empty to meet up, putting on the act of being head of the household and servant while guests are inside.

Molly is seen in 19th-century servant's clothing on the third floor of the house. She is often seen near the window from which she threw herself to end her life. Sometimes, passersby on the exterior of the building see a young lady open the window, appearing to be crying. People on the lower floors sometimes hear footsteps on the third floor when there is no one up there, and the light fixture on the third floor sometimes moves back and forth for no apparent reason.

Joseph is seen downstairs in the dining room area. He walks through the dining room, appearing as if he owns the place, looking at each table as he walks by, making sure that all of his guests are comfortable and satisfied. He is reported as being a handsome man, wearing a nice 19th-century suit.

visiting

There is dining on all three floors of the building. Joseph is most often seen on the first two floors, while Molly is seen exclusively on the third floor near one of the front windows. To enter the building, you need to be a paying customer. Prices are rather high, which is not surprising, given the place's reputation for fine dining. Entrees at dinner range from $17 to around $40, so this may not be the best place to look for ghosts if you're on a budget. If you're in the mood for some great food, stop in and maybe Joseph will check up on you. If you can't afford it, stand outside and look up to the windows on the third floor to perhaps catch a glimpse of Molly.

MABEL TAINTER THEATER

205 Main Street East, Menomonie, Wisconsin 54751

directions

From downtown St. Paul, take I-94 East for about 57 miles into Wisconsin. Take exit 41, the WI-25 exit towards Menomonie/Barron. Stay right at the fork to get onto North Broadway Street and follow that for about 2 miles. Turn left onto Main Street East and the theater will be on the left.

history

The Mabel Tainter Theater has been a center for the arts in Menomonie, Wisconsin, since it was built in 1889. Originally, the structure was created as a tribute to Mabel Tainter, a young woman from the area who loved theater and the arts. She died young at the age of 19 in 1886, and her wealthy lumber baron parents decided to construct the theater as a memorial to her. No expenses were spared in the creation of the building. The best stone from the area was used to construct the exterior façade. The designs on the walls and ceilings were created by hand. Huge stained glass masterpieces and gorgeous marble stairs and floors decorate this beautiful building. The centerpiece of the theater is a gigantic pipe organ with 1,597 pipes in the 313-seat theater auditorium.

The theater has been in constant operation since its completion and dedication in 1890 and has seen countless employees and patrons walk through its doors. The building also contained the Menomonie Public Library until 1984, when it moved to a larger building. The only remnant of the library is the Reading Room within the theater building.

ghost story

There are several places in the building where paranormal activity seems to occur. The first is the changing room area in the downstairs of the building. People have seen shadowy figures and heard phantom footsteps in this area. A paranormal group conducting an investigation in the building caught phantom voices on their audio recorders that they didn't hear at the time the recordings were made. Sometimes, people in the changing rooms feel as if they are being watched or feel generally uncomfortable.

Another haunted area in the building is the theater's auditorium, where the performances take place. Again, people see shadowy figures walking through this area, who, upon further investigation, simply disappear. The figures that appear most often are seen on the catwalks that tower over top of the stage. People see figures on the catwalks and hear voices and footsteps coming from the catwalks despite there being no one there. Other times, while actors rehearse on the stage, they see people watching them from the seats. These figures vanish. Still other times, strange things happen with the sound boards, and the organ makes noise on its own.

The most famous ghost to haunt the theater is said to be that of Mabel Tainter herself. The apparition of a woman in a white dress has often been seen floating through the building. These apparitions are seen most often on the second floor and in the women's restrooms. The apparition who appears on the second floor seems to just float by eyewitnesses. The apparition who appears in the women's restroom looks at herself in the mirror and will vanish.

visiting

There are two possible ways to visit the ghosts here. The building is open every day but Monday for self-guided tours. These tours are available from 10 a.m.–5 p.m., and many of the haunted places in the building are accessible during this tour. The other way to visit the ghosts here is to purchase tickets to the shows that are regularly performed here. The showtimes are always subject to change, and it would be best to check the theater's Web site at www.mabeltainter.com for more details.

THE MOONSHINE SALOON

1179 Seventh Street East, St. Paul, Minnesota 55106

directions

Take Seventh Street East from the heart of downtown St. Paul for about 3 miles. The bar will be on your left at the intersection of Seventh Street and Duluth Street.

history

There is a lot of history behind the building where the Moonshine Saloon sits. The building was constructed in the early 1900s and is currently more than a hundred years old. Throughout its history, it has been many things, but more recently the site has held a series of bars.

At one point in the building's history, a man hung himself to death inside. Many people who have witnessed paranormal activity here trace the activity back to this event. A while ago, the bar was named Michael's Bar, but when Michael's went out of business and new owners decided to set up a new bar at the site, they decided to reference the tragic suicide that occurred there. The name of the bar was changed from Michael's to the Noose.

ghost story

While no one has ever reported seeing an apparition within the bar, plenty of strange things have happened here. Most of the ghostly activity involves things moving around by themselves. Doors swing open and closed for no reason. Sometimes the doors open and get stuck open. People who respond to the open door have a hard time getting it to close again. Other times, a jukebox turns on and off by itself even though there is no one near it.

The activity here has also become a little aggressive. At one time, a beer glass flung itself from an empty table and shattered on the opposite wall. Another time, a neon sign mysteriously unattached itself from the wall and shattered on the floor. There was no one anywhere near the sign. The faucets in the men's restroom come on by themselves, and when someone turns them off, they turn on again.

visiting

Today, the owners of the Moonshine Saloon are not as welcoming of their ghosts as when the bar was still the Noose. The bar now serves Chinese food and is open from 4 p.m.–1 a.m. every day of the week. To experience the ghosts here, you need only go in during business hours, grab a drink or maybe some food, and observe your surroundings. Keep an eye out for flying beer mugs, though.

MOUNDS THEATER

1029 Hudson Road, St. Paul, Minnesota 55106

directions

Take Kellogg Boulevard East from the center of downtown St. Paul for about a mile until you get to Maria Avenue. Turn right onto Maria Avenue. After about a quarter mile, Maria Avenue changes its name to Hudson Road. After another half mile, the Mounds Theater will be on your left.

history

The Mounds Theater was originally constructed in 1922 and was intended as a venue where silent movies could be exhibited to the community. The building also had a stage in front of its screen to accommodate live entertainment. Several times during its years of operation, it had to undergo heavy renovations. It was renovated in 1933 and again in 1950. By the late 1960s, the business of the theater was beginning to flounder. In 1967, they finally decided the theater had completed its run, and they shut it down.

The building was used as a warehouse for the next 34 years until 2001, when people from the community decided they wanted to restore the theater. The next two years were again used for an extensive renovation project. In 2003, the theater reopened as a venue for weddings and shows as well as a movie theater.

ghost story

Typically, those who speak about the ghosts at the Mounds Theater talk about three specific ghosts who are seen here often. Shadows often flit their way through the aisles when there is no one there. Figures sit in the seats to watch the stage and screen and then will suddenly vanish. All varieties of strange sounds and figures are experienced throughout the building.

The first of this theater's famous ghosts is that of an usher dressed in a red uniform. This usher seems to act very much like a theater usher in the early 1900s would act. Sometimes he guides people to their seats. Other times, he is seen walking up and down the aisles, making sure that everything is in order.

The second ghost is that of another theater employee, a projectionist. The projectionist, of course, constantly inhabits the projection booth. Those who have seen and experienced this ghost typically have not had a pleasant experience. This projectionist seems angry and bitter and will often glare at those who see him with dark, black eyes. No one has reported a physical attack from this ghost, but people in the projection booth feel very uncomfortable and unwelcome. Sometimes aggressive and profane voices are caught on audio recordings, especially when women are present.

The third ghost is that of a little girl, who inhabits the stage area. Often she is seen skipping across the stage or bouncing a red ball. Reports often depict her as having curly blond hair and wearing a pink dress.

visiting

Throughout the year, the theater is open for movies and other shows and events. It is possible to reserve the building for weddings or other gatherings. While, during most of the year, entering the theater at these times may be your only way to experience the ghosts, there is a better way to find the ghosts during October, when they hold ghost tours during weekend nights. These ghost tours are guided by paranormal investigators, who tell the ghost stories and encourage people to take pictures and communicate with the spirits.

THE OLD JAIL BED & BREAKFAST

349 West Government Street, Taylors Falls, Minnesota 55084

directions

Take I-35E North from downtown St. Paul for about 25 miles until you reach exit 132, US-8 towards Taylors Falls. Follow US-8 for 22 miles and then turn left onto Bench Street. Take the first left onto First Street and then the first left onto West Government Street. The Old Jail Bed & Breakfast will be on your right.

history

The Old Jail Bed & Breakfast was, in fact, at one time a jail. The history of the property started much earlier than that, however. The original structure was actually a saloon built by the Schottmuller Brothers in 1869. The saloon building was connected to a cave, which ran to their brewery. The beer was brewed in their brewery and then was stored in the lower cave temperatures before being served to the men at the saloon.

In 1884, the area needed a jail, which was built directly adjacent to the saloon. Some people surmised that the reason for this was so that rowdy drunks could be more easily jailed for the night after causing a scene at the saloon.

After the building was used as a saloon, a variety of other businesses occupied the cave and the structure. At one time, the building was used as a mortuary, again utilizing the cool temperatures of the cave for preservation purposes. In 1981, the buildings on the property, including both the jail and the old saloon, were converted into the bed & breakfast, which currently occupies the property.

ghost story

As far as ghostly activity at this bed & breakfast, at least three ghosts have been experienced here. The first ghost is that of a cat. While there are no reports of anyone actually seeing a cat in the building, people sometimes report that it feels like a cat jumps into their bed in the middle of the night. When the startled lodgers get up to look for the cat, they find there is no such creature anywhere.

The other ghosts—a young boy and an older woman—have been seen together in the building. Sightings of these ghosts are often preceded by a glowing orb of light. Sometimes, the ghosts actually speak. During at least one instance, the young boy was reported to say, "Don't be afraid; we are here to watch over you."

visiting

In order to visit the ghosts here at the Old Jail Bed & Breakfast, you have to reserve a room for the night. There are several suites from which to choose: a room in the cave that once held the mortuary; a room in the jail; and a couple in the old saloon. You can choose the room in which you want to stay when making your reservations. Rooms range from $140 to $150 a night and include a breakfast, which is delivered to your door.

THE ONION GRILLE

100 Sibley Street, Hastings, Minnesota 55033

directions

Take US-61 South from downtown St. Paul for about 18 miles until you reach Hastings, Minnesota. Turn right when you get to West Third Street and then take the first right onto The Great River Road. When The Great River Road dead-ends into West Second Street, turn right and then take the second left onto Sibley Street. The Onion Grille will be on your left near Charade Lane.

history

The buildings in downtown Hastings are mostly older buildings that have been around since the 19th century. The town itself was first settled in 1851 and eventually became official in 1856. The area around Second Street, where the Onion Grille sits currently, was essentially the heart of the city. Immigrants who moved into the town lived here in the Second Street area. Any big events or pieces of history from the town typically took place in this area.

Nothing incredibly tragic seems to have occurred in the building where the Onion Grille is today, but a long history could have somehow imbued the building with its current paranormal legacy.

ghost story

Despite the lack of concrete tragedy in this historic building, a lot of ghostly activity occurs here. The most famous ghost who resides in this building is that of a 19th-century man who stands at the top of the stairs that lead to the banquet room. While employees claim to have seen this man, most of the sightings of this apparition are by children, who happen to glance up the stairs and see a man standing at the top looking down. The adults who are with these children see nothing.

Other than this apparition who is almost exclusively seen by children, many other strange things occur here that anyone can experience. Footsteps are heard in places where no one is walking. Candles light by themselves. Pictures fall off the wall without any explanation. Glasses in the bar suddenly shatter without falling. Televisions suddenly turn off by themselves, and sometimes the alarm system trips during the night, but investigators find nothing that could have set it off.

Employees have experienced some aggressive ghosts in this building. Most of these experiences happened when it was a different restaurant called the Levee Café. An employee who was in the basement alone became inexplicably locked in a storage cage. Two other employees were in the basement when suddenly their backs began to burn. Upon investigation, the employees had somehow been scratched across their backs by some unknown force.

visiting

Since the ghosts here are seen exclusively in the interior of the building, you need to enter the restaurant during normal business hours. The restaurant is open until 8 p.m. Sunday through Tuesday, until 9 p.m. Wednesday and Thursday, and until 10 p.m. on Friday and Saturday. The restaurant is not open for tours, so if you were to enter to look for the ghosts, you would need to eat a meal.

THE PEACOCK INN

314 North Walnut Street, Chaska, Minnesota 55318

directions

Take I-35W South from downtown Minneapolis for about 4 miles to exit 11, MN-62 West. Follow MN-62 for another 5.5 miles until you reach US-212 West. Follow US-212 for a little more than 12 miles until you reach the Chestnut Street exit. Turn left onto North Chestnut Street and follow it for 2 miles. Turn left onto East Fourth Street and then right onto North Walnut Street. The Peacock Inn Bed & Breakfast will be on your left.

history

The Peacock Inn was originally a lavish mansion built by State Senator Charles Klein in 1910. Charles Klein lived in the mansion with his wife, Matilda, and spared no expense in making it the most lavish home in the area. For many years, the Kleins lived in the house and loved it. They lived in the house until they died.

Eventually, the house became the property of the Bohns, who currently run the building as a bed & breakfast. When they started the bed & breakfast, they took special care to restore the house to the opulence and luxury it exhibited in the early 1900s. Apparently, the décor isn't the only thing that harkens back to an earlier time in the building's history.

ghost story

Several strange things happen in this bed & breakfast. A rocking chair in Room 3 rocks by itself. Anyone who witnesses the strange occurrence looks desperately for a cause for the rocking but is always disappointed. In Rooms 4 and 5, people have seen a woman dancing through their room and past their doorway. When they investigate this strange dancing woman, they find no physical sign of her anywhere.

These aren't the only strange happenings in this century-old building. A ghost cat supposedly haunts the building. It is seen roaming the house and sometimes jumps up onto the bed as visitors are comfortably asleep for the evening. The owner does not own any cats and is in fact allergic to them.

Things throughout the house inexplicably move around as well. The owners set the table the night before for the next morning's breakfast but awaken to find all the silverware has been put away. The owners also once attempted to hang a mirror in one of the rooms by driving a nail into the plaster and hanging the mirror from it. The mirror fell unbroken to the floor beside the nail, and the wall had no hole where the nail had been driven in.

visiting

This building is an operating bed & breakfast, so the best chance of encountering any of the friendly spirits is to rent a room for the night. The owners do not market the place as a haunted bed & breakfast but instead market it as a place where you can experience the elegance of the early 20th century. It has been voted one of the most romantic getaway locations in the area by a local newspaper. Go ahead, get yourself a room in the haunted mansion and say hi to one of the friendly spirits that reside there.

PIZZA HUT

3854 Central Avenue Northeast, Columbia Heights,
Minnesota 55421

directions

Take Third Street South across the Mississippi River from downtown Minneapolis.
Once across the river, the road changes its name to Central Avenue Northeast. Follow
Central Avenue Northeast for a little more than 4 miles. Since Pizza Hut will be on
the left-hand side of a divided road, you'll need to make a U-turn in order to reach
the restaurant.

history

The ghost here can trace its origin to the business that was in the building before Pizza
Hut. Before this was a Pizza Hut, it was a donut shop, which was a favorite destination
for many people in the area.

One of the bakers who worked at the donut shop fell upon hard times and became
quite depressed. Since he often entered the shop before it was open in order to start
making the donuts, he was the only one in the building when he killed himself. He
set up a noose in the back area of the donut shop and hung himself. His body wasn't
found until another employee showed up later that morning.

ghost story

The baker who killed himself is seen from time to time. Most of the time, the apparition is seen in the morning, and since the building doesn't open to the public until 10:45 a.m., employees are usually the only ones who get a chance to see him. People see a man in a white apron walking around the restaurant absently. Sometimes, he is seen by customers who show up early for lunch, but this only occurs when the building is not crowded and the customers are the only ones in the building.

Other strange things happen in the restaurant. Sometimes the lights in the main dining room turn off by themselves in the middle of the day. Other lights inside the building turn on and off for no reason during any time of day or night. Water faucets in the kitchens and the restrooms will turn on by themselves as well.

visiting

To see this ghost, you have to enter the building during regular business hours unless you're an employee. The restaurant opens at 10:45 each morning and is open until midnight every day of the week. The best time to see the apparition of the baker is when the restaurant opens at 10:45. The light and faucet phenomena have been known to occur at any time of the day or night, so if you just wanted to grab a bite to eat in a haunted restaurant, stop in any time and you may just experience something.

REGAL CINEMAS BROOKLYN CENTER

6420 Camden Avenue North, Brooklyn Center, Minnesota 55430

directions

Take I-94 West from downtown Minneapolis for 4.5 miles to MN-252 North. A little more than a half mile after merging onto MN-252 North, turn left onto 66th Avenue North. Turn left onto Camden Avenue, and the movie theater will be on your left.

history

This immense 20-screen multiplex was built just outside of Minneapolis in 2000. An accident during the construction of the theater has continued to haunt this place for more than a decade. A man was working on the roof near where theater 10 is today when the accident occurred. He lost his footing and fell off the high roof to the concrete sidewalk below and died from injuries sustained during the fall.

The theater itself opened in September of 2000 and has been entertaining audiences since that time.

ghost story

The ghost stories in this building seem to focus around theater 10. Since this is where the man fell to his death during construction, those who have experienced the ghost assume it is the ghost of this man.

In the theater before the movie starts or even during the movie, patrons have felt a presence in the auditorium with them. They either hear footsteps walking up and down the aisles, or they suddenly feel certain there is someone sitting directly behind them but turn around and find no one there. Employees and managers in the projection booth have experienced similar sensations. Footsteps are often heard although there is no one else there. Other loud noises like something falling have occurred in the projection booth, but no matter how hard the employees search, nothing seems to have fallen.

visiting

Your best bet for finding a ghost at the Regal Cinemas is to go to a movie playing in theater 10. You may need to ask the cashier which movie is playing in theater 10, but they would have access to that information. The best time to go is a time that is not busy. This is your best chance to sit in the theater alone and experience those feelings that you are not actually alone.

Unfortunately, in order to access the projection booth, you have to be an employee or a manager at the theater.

SAINT PAUL HOTEL

350 Market Street, St. Paul, Minnesota 55102

directions

Take North Market Street towards Fifth Street East from the heart of St. Paul, Minnesota. Standing just a couple of blocks away from the Mississippi River, the hotel takes up most of the block between North Market Street and St. Peter Street at Fifth Street East.

history

Hotels operated on this property as early as 1856. An early resident of the city simply invited visitors to stay with him at his house at the site. Eventually, he realized that creating a hotel at the site would be lucrative because of the influx of visitors into the growing town. In 1871, he built a 60-room hotel at the site, and for the next seven years, the hotel did quite well. In 1878, though, the hotel caught fire and burned to the ground, killing several patrons who were unable to escape the burning building in time.

In 1880, a new hotel, the Windsor, was opened at the site. Again, the hotel went out of business several years later. In 1904, the hotel was turned into a theater and arcade complex that operated for two years before people in the city realized the need for a luxury hotel in the rapidly growing St. Paul area. By 1910, the Saint Paul Hotel was built and was the most luxurious hotel in the state.

Throughout the hundred years of its existence, many famous people have stayed at the hotel, including Charles Lindbergh and John F. Kennedy. For a while, the mafia boss of St. Paul, Leon Gleckman, ran his illegal operations from a suite in the hotel. Many a murder was likely planned within these walls.

By the 1950s, the hotel was starting to deteriorate as business was moving away from the heart of the city. The hotel continued to deteriorate until the 1980s when they decided they would refurbish the hotel and restore it to what it once was. Today, the hotel is again one of the most luxurious and beautiful hotels in the city.

ghost story

Several ghosts have been reported within the walls of this historic hotel—some of them are a little unsettling. Guests on some of the lower floors have reported waking up in the middle of the night to the sound of doors in their rooms closing by themselves. Other times, lights or televisions turn on without anyone touching them. Perhaps the most unsettling ghost is that of a burned man, his flesh apparently blackened by fire, who is seen walking the hallways on the lower levels. Sometimes, the man is seen within hotel rooms in the middle of the night.

While these ghosts can be unsettling, the sightings of these ghosts are quite rare. One ghost, though, is frequently encountered throughout the hotel. The ghost takes the form of a bellboy and is actually quite helpful. He aids visitors by carrying their bags or answering questions about the hotel or the surrounding area. He wears a uniform that appears to be from the early 20th century. Sometimes, visitors don't even realize the bellboy is a ghost until he suddenly leaves their room without opening the door, or he just suddenly vanishes from sight.

visiting

While it is possible to enter the hotel to dine at one of its elegant restaurants or to simply view the gorgeous lobby, to have a chance at encountering the ghosts here, you need to rent a room for the night. If you are doing your paranormal exploration on a limited budget, this particular hotel may be a little out of your price range. The cheapest rooms in the hotel are around $189, and the more expensive ones can be as pricey as $264.

ST JAMES HOTEL

406 Main Street, Red Wing, Minnesota 55066

directions

From downtown St. Paul, take Warner Road for a little more than 2 miles and then turn right onto US-10 East. Follow US-10 East for a little more than 16 miles before turning left to stay on US-10. Follow US-10 for another 3 miles into Wisconsin and then turn right onto Broad Street/WI-35. Follow WI-35 for about 20 miles before turning right onto US-63 to cross back into Minnesota. After another 3 miles, turn right onto Plum Street and then take the first left onto West Main Street. The St. James Hotel will be on your right.

history

As Red Wing was becoming a busy town due to the large lumber businesses in the area, business leaders in the town decided they needed a grand hotel to accommodate the increasing number of tourists and visitors to Red Wing. In 1874, work began on the hotel. As if some kind of omen towards its haunted future, work was soon halted. Human remains were dug up as they had started work on the hotel. Apparently, the site they had chosen had been a Native American burial ground. The bodies were moved and construction continued.

On Thanksgiving in 1875, the hotel had its grand opening celebration. It has been in constant operation since this time. Ownership of the building has changed several times during its long history. Perhaps the most noteworthy owner was a woman named Clara Lillyblad, who started as a waitress in the hotel but eventually married the owner. When her husband died, Clara took over ownership of the hotel and was closely involved with all aspects of the hotel's operation. The hotel became her life until she died in 1977.

Today, the hotel is still a grand hotel, which offers rooms, dining, and a venue for parties or weddings. It also seems to house some paranormal memories of its long history.

ghost story

Each section of this immense building is haunted by what seems to be its own paranormal entity. The Victorian Dining Room is haunted by unexplained voices and feelings. An old table in one room was apparently there when Clara was still there, and she doesn't like it moved. When people attempt to move it, they feel an inexplicable force pushing back at them. The lobby is haunted by strange shadows that vanish as quickly as they appear. Rooms 310 and 311 are haunted by the ghost of Clara herself. People see her apparition floating through these rooms and then vanishing. People feel uncomfortable and feel or see a male presence in the basement. Sometimes people see floating lights moving through the Port of Red Wing Restaurant in the basement.

The second-floor offices are haunted by what seems to be a child. An employee returned to her work area and found a note on her desk that appeared to have been written by a child, which said, "Who are you?" The third-floor offices are haunted by a little girl in a white dress, who runs through the offices and vanishes without a trace. People also see a little girl roaming through many of the hallways in the large hotel.

Finally, the main stairway is haunted. People climbing or descending the stairway sometimes feel as if they are drowning. They are suddenly unable to breath.

It seems as if many remnants of the hotel's long past have remained here and still lurk in the hotel's many rooms and corridors.

visiting

If you cannot afford the time or money to spend the night in this haunted hotel, you have the option of entering in hopes of finding some of the resident ghosts. There are restaurants and a pub on site that you can enter without having a room reservation, and there are some shops to browse.

Your best bet for finding the ghosts here, however, is to rent a room for the night. Try Rooms 310 and 311, since these were Clara's rooms during her life.

WATER STREET INN

101 Water Street South, Stillwater, Minnesota 55082

directions

From downtown St. Paul, take I-35E North for about 4 miles to exit 111A. Take MN-36 East towards Stillwater and follow this road for 16.5 miles to South Main Street. After the highway changes its name to South Main Street, take the first right onto South Myrtle Street. The inn is on the corner of Water Street and Myrtle Street, just before you get to the river.

history

This building was constructed during the boom years of the logging business in 1890. Many people in Minnesota made a lot of money during the years when logging was lucrative in the area. A select few, nicknamed the lumber barons, became incredibly rich during this time, and they had a large part in building this place. It originally contained many amenities that were unheard of in 1890. There was electricity, heating, and even an elevator in the building. The barons lived in the building, and each floor had a large walk-in vault in which these men could store their fortunes. After the lumber boom ended in the 1910s, the lumber barons abandoned the property. It was then used by local lawyers and businessmen as office and living space.

During the early days of the building's existence, a former soldier who fought for the Confederacy during the Civil War was staying in a suite on the second floor of the building on the northwest corner. He had been drinking quite heavily at the downstairs bar all evening. When he returned to the room, he succumbed to alcohol poisoning and died in the room.

ghost story

There are two places in this building that seem to be hotbeds of paranormal activity. The first is the room on the second floor in the northwest corner. The most often reported phenomenon here is that people encounter phantom smells, like heavy sweat or alcohol, and then the smells suddenly dissipate. Other times, doors close and faucets turn on and off for no reason.

The other haunted location in the building is the downstairs bar called Charlie's. Glasses move across tables without anything pushing them. People hear the sounds of

chairs scooting across the floor in an area where no one is sitting and nothing appears to be moving. People also hear phantom footsteps in the bar when there is no one walking around.

visiting

Visiting the ghosts at the pub is much easier than visiting the ghost in the hotel room. Just enter the pub during normal business hours to have a chance at finding the ghosts here. To get into the haunted room, though, you have to reserve the second-floor northwest corner room and stay the night there. Although this is not impossible to do, it is more expensive and requires more forethought than simply walking into the haunted pub.

SECTION V

schools and public places

ANOKA CITY HALL

2015 First Avenue North, Anoka, Minnesota 55303

directions

From downtown Minneapolis, take I-94 North for about 4.5 miles to MN-252 North. Follow MN-252 for another 4 miles and then merge onto MN-610 West. Follow MN-610 for about 4.5 more miles and then merge onto US-169 North. Follow US-169 for 5 miles and then turn right onto Main Street. Turn left onto North Second Avenue, then take the first left onto Jackson Street. Jackson Street will lead you directly into the city hall parking lot at the corner of First Avenue North.

history

The City Hall building wasn't constructed until the 1950s. It was funded by a company called Federal Cartridge, which manufactured guns and ammunition. Perhaps as homage to the benefactor, the building was shaped like a handgun. If you were to look at the building from the air, the layout of the building closely resembles a gun.

The ghosts likely have little to do with City Hall itself. The area where City Hall was built was once a grain mill called the Washburn Mill. At the end of the 19th century, the mill suffered a catastrophe. An explosion rocked the mill, and the building burned to the ground. Many were killed in the accident. According to stories told about the incident, a woman whose husband worked in the mill rushed to the site to find out whether or not her husband was a casualty of the explosion. For the next eight hours, she waited breathlessly to hear the fate of her husband. Finally, she learned that her husband had indeed been killed in the blast.

ghost story

The most haunted area in the building is the second floor, especially in the area that represents the barrel of the gun. Those who have experienced or heard about the ghostly happenings here, suggest that the ghost of the woman whose husband was killed in the mill explosion continues to roam the City Hall building. People waiting in line at a clerk's office on the second floor have suddenly been shoved violently from behind by some unseen force. Once, the victim was actually pushed forward onto a clerk's desk. Others have reported extreme feelings of discomfort in the women's restroom on the second floor. Some employees in the building actually avoid this closer restroom and go all the way across the building to a further yet less discomforting restroom.

Others hear phantom footsteps throughout the building. Doors close and lock themselves at all times of the day or night; sometimes locked doors mysteriously become unlocked for no reason.

visiting

Anoka City Hall is a public building, so you are allowed to enter during regular business hours. You do have access to both the haunted second floor by the clerk's office and, if you are female, the women's restroom on the second floor. Go ahead and tour the building and maybe you'll just get a little shove as you're walking down a second-floor hallway.

BURNSVILLE CENTER

1083 Burnsville Center, Burnsville, Minnesota 55306

directions

From downtown Minneapolis, take I-35W South for a little more than 15 miles to exit 1, Crystal Lake Road. You'll be able to see the giant mall from the highway but stay straight past CR-42 until you come to an entrance road to the mall. Turn right into the mall and park anywhere. The ghost is inside.

history

Burnsville Center is a giant shopping mall just outside of the Twin Cities in a town called Burnsville. The original idea for the mall was conceived when Homart Development decided they wanted to lease out a large shopping area to vendors just outside of the major metropolitan areas of Minneapolis and St. Paul. A man named Joe Rimnac sold his farmland to the developers, and construction began on one of the largest malls in the world.

While the shopping mall itself has always been intended as a place to shop and have fun, it is not entirely without tragedy. During construction, a man was working on the building's high walls. The section of wall that was his responsibility required scaffolding to reach, so he was several stories above the ground as he worked. He somehow got tripped up on that scaffolding and tragically fell to his death to the floor below.

ghost story

The ghost of the man who fell to his death inside the mall still haunts this building. The ghost exhibits himself most frequently through sound. Many times, people who are relatively alone in some corner of the mall hear what sound like footsteps on metal scaffolding. Upon further investigation, there is nothing nearby that could be causing the sounds. Perhaps the sounds are just replays of the construction worker's final moments.

An apparition of the construction worker himself is sometimes seen in the mall as well. The apparition is much rarer and is only seen near the times when the building opens or closes. Witnesses see a man dressed as a construction worker with shoulder-length brown hair and a mustache walking through the building. He is always wearing a construction worker's helmet and actually appears quite normal. Surprisingly, though, this construction worker suddenly turns and walks right through a wall as if it were not there.

visiting

There is not a specific part of the building the ghost haunts. The ghost seems to roam throughout the entire building, even sometimes wandering into stores. The thing about the haunting that is common throughout all the stories is that the ghost manifests when the witness is relatively alone. If you want to find the ghost inside this building, find yourself a secluded place and listen for the footsteps. The apparition is seen at opening, around 10 a.m., and is sometimes seen at closing, around 9 p.m.

COUNTY HIGHWAY 22 IN LINWOOD

Viking Boulevard Northeast between Typo Creek Drive and
197th Avenue, Wyoming, Minnesota 55092

directions

From downtown St. Paul, take I-35E North for about 27.5 miles to exit 135, the
Wyoming exit. Turn left at the end of the exit ramp. This will put you on County
Highway 22, which is also known as Viking Boulevard Northeast. After about 5.5
miles on this stretch, you'll reach the haunted section of the road. The haunted
section is through Linwood between Typo Creek Drive and 197th Avenue.

history

While this quiet stretch of road connecting Wyoming, Linwood, and East Bethel may
seem safe and unassuming, a remarkable number of accidents have occurred along
it. More surprisingly still, most of the accidents that have happened here are single-
car accidents. Sometimes, for inexplicable reasons, a car will just lose control and
crash, killing all onboard. Drivers suddenly roll their cars driving down this reasonably
straight road.

Authorities blame the accidents on people exceeding the speed limit on this dark
country road. Some survivors blame something else entirely.

ghost story

Some of those people who survive accidents along this dangerous stretch of road say they were swerving in order to avoid a young woman who was walking down the middle of the westbound lane of the road. They always say she was wearing a thin dress and was covered with blood. As the witnesses are speeding down the road, they are unable to see the woman until it's too late. They swerve to miss her and often wreck their cars. When they get out of their cars and look for the young woman, she is nowhere to be found.

Sightings of the young woman in the thin, bloody dress happen throughout the year, but they happen most frequently in the fall during September and October.

visiting

This location is a mixed blessing for ghost hunters. On the one hand, it is a public road open at all times. You could traverse this road at any time of the day or night. Later in the evening, this road seems rather remote and creepy, so you can drive up and down it throughout the night, looking for the ghost of the bloody woman.

On the other hand, though, this is a dangerous road, especially for those who are not paying close attention. Make sure that if you are driving up and down this road, you are very careful. Remember, many accidents have occurred here. Don't add yourself to the ghost's victims.

FALCON RIDGE MIDDLE SCHOOL

12900 Johnny Cake Ridge Road, Apple Valley,
Minnesota 55124

directions

From St. Paul, follow I-35E South for about 13.5 miles until you reach exit 93, the
Cliff Road exit. Follow Cliff Road for about a mile before turning right onto Johnny
Cake Ridge Road. After about 2 miles on Johnny Cake Ridge Road, the middle school
will be on your left.

history

The Falcon Ridge Middle School building was constructed in 1995 in the city of
Apple Valley. A rather dark and strange story circulates about the construction process
of the building itself. As a large hole was being dug for the foundation of the school,
one of the construction workers somehow fell into the hole and was buried alive.
Before anyone realized the man was missing, they poured concrete into the foundation
and further buried the construction worker.

By the time everyone realized what must have happened to the worker, it was
far too late. They would have had to destroy all the work they had already done and
perhaps would not have even then found the poor man's body. So they left it there.

ghost story

The school is haunted by the ghost of the construction worker who was buried alive
during the school's construction. Luckily for the children who attend the school during
the day, the ghost seems to only show himself at night.

People who are near the school at night, sometimes see a shadowy figure wondering absently through the grounds of the school. If the figure is ever approached, he suddenly disappears without a trace. Sometimes people hear moaning coming from the school grounds after dark, and to the annoyance of those who work at the school, sometimes the ghost opens locked doors in the middle of the night. When the staff shows up with the police in the middle of the night to investigate the alarms having gone off, nothing is found but an open door.

Strange things also happen with the lights in and around the school late at night. Sometimes, the lights inside the building mysteriously come on. Sometimes they actually flash on and off throughout the whole school. The lights on the adjacent street and in the schoolyard come on and go off for no reason as well.

visiting

Usually, when you have a haunted school, the ghosts are only accessible to those who attend and those who work at the school. This school is an exception to this rule because most of the ghostly phenomena occur in a way that can be observed from the school's exterior. You can drive by the school and maybe see the ghost walking through the schoolyard. You can watch for mysterious lights and listen for mysterious moaning.

The one thing you need to keep in mind when looking for this ghost is to make sure you do not trespass onto school property after dark. If you are caught trespassing, especially on those nights when the alarms go off in the school, you will be arrested. It's best to just observe the school from the road that runs past it.

HAMLINE UNIVERSITY DREW HALL

1539 Hewitt Avenue, St. Paul, Minnesota 55104

directions

From downtown St. Paul, take I-94 West for about 3 miles to exit 238 toward Snelling Avenue. At the end of the exit ramp, turn right onto Snelling Avenue. Follow Snelling Avenue for 1 mile until you see Hewitt Avenue. Turn right onto Hewitt Avenue. About halfway onto the university's campus, you'll see Drew Hall on your left. There will be a sign in front.

history

While Hamline University itself is the oldest university in the Minnesota, Drew Hall is relatively new in comparison. The hall was built in the mid-1900s and has existed since that time as a residence hall, classroom building, and administrative office building. Today, the building houses all of these things as well as student lounges and an auditorium. It was named after a benefactor of the university, a lawyer named Charles Drew.

The ghost story stems from an accident that occurred in the school during the 1960s. Soon after the elevator was installed in the hall, a young freshman student thought it wise to show off in front of his friends. He put his hand in the closing doors of the elevator seconds before it slammed closed, counting on the sensors in the door to cause the doors to spring back open. This worked several times, but then he cut it too close. He put his hand into the elevator without giving the sensors enough time to register his hand, and his hand was severed.

The student survived but his hand was never found.

ghost story

Believe it or not, Drew Hall is haunted by a hand. Most of the stories about this ghostly hand involve people actually seeing it crawling through dark corridors and stairwells of the building. According to the legends about this phantom hand, it has somehow developed a mind of its own and is crawling around the building looking for the body from which it was detached.

While stories of a hand walking around the hall may seem unfeasible and blown out of proportion, other stories tell a different version of how the phantom hand haunts the hall. Residents at Drew Hall, especially females, sometimes feel icy cold fingers touching their feet at night. When they awake suddenly and in terror, they look and find no one else is in the room.

visiting

It is possible for a visitor from outside the campus to enter Drew Hall. Since the building houses administrative offices and classrooms, the doors from the outside are open, and you can enter parts of the building. That being said, though, this is a place of learning and a professional establishment. You should not enter Drew Hall with the sole intention of looking for ghosts. As a student or employee, you can enter, but if you are not, the university would frown upon you entering the building.

To have any chance of experiencing the icy cold fingers on your feet at night, you would have to be both female and a resident of the hall.

HAMLINE UNIVERSITY OLD MAIN BUILDING

1536 Hewitt Avenue, St. Paul, Minnesota 55104

directions

From downtown St. Paul, take I-94 West for about 3 miles to exit 238 toward Snelling Avenue. At the end of the exit ramp, turn right onto Snelling Avenue. Follow Snelling Avenue for 1 mile until you see Hewitt Avenue. Turn right onto Hewitt Avenue. About halfway onto the campus on your right, you will see the large bell tower of the Old Main Building.

history

When the University moved to St. Paul in 1873, a grand, central university building was constructed. This building held all school functions and classes and operated as the center of the school. In 1883, tragedy struck as the building caught fire and burned to the ground. The very next year, 1884, the new building that still stands today was constructed.

Originally, the Old Main Building housed the majority of the university's functions. All of the university's classrooms were inside the building. Also, administrative offices and a dining hall were located here. The auditorium that is now inside of the building was named after one of the men instrumental in the success of the school, university president George Henry Bridgman. Bridgman Auditorium was originally a chapel and would become a lecture hall and eventually a music hall in its later years. President William McKinley once gave a speech at the hall. In September of 1985, fire again struck the building, this time originating within Bridgman Auditorium. While no one was hurt in the fire, extensive renovations had to be done to repair the hall.

Today, there is a painting of George Henry Bridgman hanging in the auditorium.

ghost story

The Old Main Building at Hamline University has its share of ghostly activity. One particularly strange entity is said to often roam the halls of this place. At first, when the apparition is spotted, the witness thinks there is just a student walking through the halls. Upon closer examination, though, they see the student isn't walking at all. The apparition is floating slightly above the floor, and he appears to have a noose tied around his neck.

There are also reports that say that goblins roam the halls of this old building. Little mischievous creatures are seen ducking around corners and causing mayhem. These goblins do anything, from pushing stacks of paper onto the ground to spilling coffee all over delicate electronics.

The most famous ghost at the Old Main Building is the ghost of George Henry Bridgman himself. The stories are quite strange, and they tend to focus around his portrait that hangs in the auditorium. According to the legends, Bridgman's portrait comes to life. Sometimes he simply watches you as you walk past him. Other times, he actually steps out of his painting and walks around. Sometimes he even plays the piano in the auditorium.

visiting

Since this building houses university administrative offices, it is difficult to enter the building to explore without being enrolled at the school or employed by the school. Sometimes, there are lectures or events open to the public in the Bridgman Auditorium, but these events are few and far between. Unfortunately, your best bet for exploring the paranormal side of this building is to actually go to the school itself.

JOHNSON MEMORIAL DRIVE

19500 Johnson Memorial Drive, Jordan, Minnesota 55352

directions

From downtown Minneapolis, take I-35W South for a little more than 7 miles until you reach I-494 West at exit 9B. Follow I-494 for about 5 miles until you reach exit 10B, US-169 South. Follow US-169 South the rest of the way. You will reach Jordan after about 23 miles. Between Jordan and Belle Plaine is the haunted stretch of road. Keep your eyes on the train tracks that will be on your right.

history

This area has been settled by Europeans since the mid-1800s. The towns grew along the train tracks and trails, which entered and exited the nearby city of Minneapolis. Throughout their long history, these railroad tracks have been used by countless trains moving countless supplies and people through the area. The entire area was typical of little towns in the Midwest.

ghost story

Along US-169 in this stretch between Jordan and Belle Plaine, people often see shadow figures. Most often, these shadowy figures are seen on the railroad tracks. These figures are never carrying lights and are never around in broad daylight. This makes the window where these figures are visible rather small. Dusk is typically the time when these figures are seen—it's not too dark to see them, and it's not too bright for them to be out.

The figures aren't just seen along the railroad tracks, though. Sometimes the figures approach the road too. In these cases, the figures are seen all throughout the night. From time to time, these figures are seen walking across the road. When headlights from an oncoming car hit them, witnesses are shocked to realize the figures are translucent and seem to dissipate as the oncoming cars pass through them. Perhaps the creepiest incarnation these shadowy figures take is that they will stand along the side of the road, just staring emptily at passing vehicles. Witnesses see these figures staring at them from the side of the road, so they slow down so as not to hit them if they were to choose to cross, but as these passing cars slow down, the figures vanish.

visiting

This road is a public road open throughout the night. The railroad tracks, though, are private property owned by the railroad company, which does not want anyone walking on the tracks, especially at night. It is far too dangerous for anyone to wander near train tracks.

LANDMARK CENTER

75 West Fifth Street, St. Paul, Minnesota 55102

directions

Landmark Center is in the heart of downtown St. Paul. It takes up an entire city block between Fifth and Sixth Streets and between Market and Washington Streets. The building has a large clock tower and many other turrets across its steep roof. The exterior is granite, and it is difficult to miss.

history

The Landmark Center was constructed in the late 1800s to serve as a home for St. Paul's post office and court system. Many famous gangsters from the early 1900s went through the court system here at the Landmark Center. Eventually, the post office and court system were moved elsewhere, and the building was scheduled to be destroyed. Concerned citizens petitioned to have the building saved, and it has today been restored to its original brilliance. It houses several museums and a historical society.

Perhaps one of the lesser-known stories involves a convicted murderer named Jack Peifer. Jack was a gangster with a local organized crime syndicate who was caught and convicted of murder. He was sentenced to 30 years at Leavenworth prison but wasn't willing to accept his fate. Before they moved him from the Landmark Center to his new home at Leavenworth, he killed himself. According to many reports, he still hasn't left the building.

ghost story

The ghost of Jack Peifer seems to have some fun terrorizing people who visit the Landmark Center today. The place where he is seen most often is in the elevators. People enter the elevator with him and then glance back to find that he has vanished. Other times, people in the elevators hear laughter coming from behind them and then look to find themselves alone. Still other times, the elevators go up and down by themselves without anyone inside.

Jack is also encountered from time to time in the women's restroom on the second floor. Besides his apparition manifesting in the restroom, the stall doors swing open and slam shut by themselves, and toilets flush by themselves.

When celebrations are held at the Landmark Center, Jack often tends to make an appearance. Glasses of alcohol tip over, people are touched by some unseen force, and a strange man, whom no one remembers seeing at the party but who resembles old Jack Peifer himself, appears in photographs of the event.

visiting

The building is often open to the public until 5 p.m. every day of the week except Thursday when it is open until 8 p.m. Remember that the hot spots for the paranormal activity here are the elevators and the women's restroom on the second floor. These places are accessible to the public at any time during these normal business hours.

Special events are free and often take place at the Landmark Center. Sometimes these special events occur after the building would otherwise be closed, so they are your only opportunity to enter the building later on in the night. These events change times throughout the course of the year, so you have to check the building's Web site at www.landmarkcenter.org to find out exactly what and when these events are.

MALL OF AMERICA

8100 S 24th Avenue, Bloomington, Minnesota 55425

directions

From downtown Minneapolis, take I-35W South for about 4 miles to exit 11, the MN-62 East exit. Follow MN-62 East for about 2 miles and then merge onto MN-77 South at Cedar Avenue. Follow MN-77 for another 2 miles and then take the Killebrew Drive exit. Stay straight onto Killebrew Drive and then take your first left into the Mall of America parking area.

history

The Mall of America, the largest mall in the United States, opened its doors on August 11, 1992. It was built on the original site of Metropolitan Stadium, where the Twins and Vikings had once played. In fact, there is a plaque in the current amusement park area of the mall that designates the area where home plate once was. Surprisingly, since this is a shopping mall that has only been open for 20 years, there has been a lot of death in this building and in the surrounding parking garages.

Some of the deadlier areas in the mall are the escalators by the upstairs bars. On multiple occasions, drunk bar patrons have lost their balance and fallen down multiple stories to their deaths. Sometimes it takes months to clean up all of the blood in the cracks of the tile. Another man was climbing the railing in the fourth floor rotunda when he slipped and fell to his death. Others have committed suicide within the mall and the adjacent parking garages, including a homeless man who killed himself in one of the parking garages. His body was never identified and was eventually buried as an unknown male.

A significant amount of violence has also occurred within the building. Many muggings and sexual assaults have been committed in the building's many restrooms. There have also been shootings and kidnappings in the building. Perhaps the most remembered shooting was when someone was shot over a Starter jacket in one of the mall's stores.

ghost story

It is no wonder, with the amount of violence and tragedy that has occurred here, paranormal activity has been left behind. The stories we came across most often when inquiring about ghosts tended to involve the mall's restrooms. Faucets come on by themselves, or stall doors swing open or shut despite the restroom being completely empty.

Another commonly experienced phenomenon here involves any of the building's elevators. People report that the elevator doors open for them, despite not having hit any buttons and no one being on the elevator. Near opening or closing time, when there are few patrons left in the building, people also report phantom footsteps following them down long corridors and, again, in the restrooms.

People also hear voices at night coming from closed stores where all the lights have been turned off. When these voices are further investigated, there is no sign anyone was ever there.

visiting

Despite all the death that has occurred in the building, it is quite safe. The suicides, murders, and kidnappings were isolated incidents that happened infrequently throughout the mall's 20-year history. The mall has become safer as well compared to when it first opened. It is the busiest mall in the country, though, so you still need to exercise a reasonable amount of caution.

Stores are open at the Mall of America Monday through Saturday, 10 a.m.–9:30 p.m., and Sunday, 11–7 p.m., but the building itself is open much later than that. Movie theaters and bars are open until midnight or even later. If you are there to experience the mall itself and not just the ghostly happenings here, you can certainly arrive at any time during regular retail hours. If you are just here for the ghosts, though, your best bet is to come after most of the patrons have left at 9:30. At this time, the mall is quieter and more suited to those looking for ghosts. The restrooms are probably the most haunted places in the building.

MINNEAPOLIS CITY HALL

350 South Fifth Street, Minneapolis, Minnesota 55415

directions

City Hall is located in the heart of downtown Minneapolis on Fifth Street between Third and Fourth Avenues South. It is a large stone building with a green copper roof. The building is accentuated by a large clock tower.

history

This incarnation of Minneapolis's City Hall was constructed when the original City Hall was razed to make way for Gateway Park. The city did not hold back when designing the impressive building. In 1912 they finished the giant structure, but the building was in use as early as 1895. The entire exterior was built from granite, and the clock tower was the tallest structure in Minnesota until the 1920s. The clock itself was billed as the largest clock face in the world at the time, with a diameter bigger than that of Big Ben.

The building was used as a courthouse, and part of it was actually used as a prison. In 1898, a man named John Moshik was held in the prison for a robbery and murder he had committed. He pled "inherited insanity," claiming that he had attained his murderous tendencies from his father. The court convicted him of murder and hung him at the gallows that had been built within the building. His neck didn't break, so it took him several minutes to slowly strangle to death. He was the last man the state of Minnesota hung. He had stolen only $14 in the robbery.

ghost story

While the entire building encompasses a wealth of history and importance to the city, it is the upper floors that reputedly house the building's infamous ghost. Those who have witnessed the ghostly activity in this building claim the ghost is none other than John Moshik himself.

On the fifth floor, people often are overcome by feelings of fear and dread and are unable to determine why they suddenly feel this way. People walking down the hallways on the fourth and fifth floors report hearing the sounds of footsteps following them down the hallways. When they turn to see who is walking behind them, the hallway is completely empty. Icy breezes often inexplicably blow through the hallways on the fifth floor. Other witnesses have actually seen an apparition of a man dressed in black floating through the hallways and then suddenly vanishing.

The actual location where Moshik was hung is also reputed to be haunted in much the same way. The gallows were in the area that is today the staff dining room and laundry room. Staff members in these rooms often see an apparition that takes one of two forms. Sometimes, Moshik takes the form of a man staring blankly, wearing nothing but boxer shorts. Other times, people actually witness the apparition of Moshik hanging by a noose from the ceiling.

visiting

Since it is a public building, most of it is open to the public. The hallways on the fifth floor are open to the public to explore while the building is in operation during the day, but the rooms on the floor are occupied mostly by offices and cannot be entered by the public. The staff dining room and laundry room are off limits to the public, so unless you work for the city, you may not get a chance to see the ghosts in these locations.

MINNEAPOLIS COLLEGE OF ART AND DESIGN

2501 Stevens Avenue, Minneapolis, Minnesota 55404

directions

From downtown Minneapolis, take South Third Street for about a mile and a half to E 22nd Street. Turn right onto 22nd Street and then take the first left onto Stevens Avenue. The campus for the Minneapolis College of Art and Design will be on your left.

history

While the college itself was founded in 1883, the facilities themselves didn't move to their present location until 1911. The college was housed in a museum for the first few years until a more permanent building could be constructed. Throughout its many years of operation, the Minneapolis College of Art and Design has been the home to many famous artists and is considered one of the best colleges for art in the entire country.

A bit of darker history exists within the walls of this important college. In the late 1980s, a tragic event happened in the student living facility. Seven apartment buildings are located on campus, giving students an opportunity to live on school grounds while they are attaining their degrees. In the late 1980s, a young female student was raped and murdered in one of the basement apartments on campus. Apparently, her ghost haunts the whole campus.

ghost story

Most of the hauntings take place in the apartment buildings on campus. Female students who are living in these buildings sometimes awake in the middle of the night with the sensation that someone is holding them down. For several terrifying minutes, the students will be unable to move. When they are finally released and able to move, they find there is no one else in their apartment. Other times, people in the apartment complexes hear deafening screams coming from somewhere else in the building. When they go to investigate, they find no one else had even heard the screaming.

Within the classrooms of the school, items will strangely go missing. People who swear they left something in a particular location return the next day to find it has gone missing. Doors in the school building sometimes open and close by themselves, even on days when there is relatively no wind.

visiting

Unfortunately, to visit the apartment buildings on campus, you would either have to be a student who lives in one or friends with a student who lives there. Otherwise, these buildings are off limits to the public. The only areas of the campus accessible to the public are the outdoor areas between buildings. We have not come across any ghost stories in these areas, though.

MINNESOTA STATE CAPITOL

75 Rev. Dr. Martin Luther King Jr. Boulevard, St. Paul,
Minnesota 55155

directions

The Minnesota State Capitol building is in the heart of downtown St. Paul on a hill
overlooking the city. From I-94, take the Marion Street exit and turn towards Aurora
Avenue (if eastbound turn left, if westbound turn right.) Turn right onto Aurora. The
capitol building is one block away and is impossible to miss.

history

The first state capitol building was taken down by a fire in 1881, immediately leaving a
symbolic void at the heart of Minnesota government. Two years later, a second capitol
building was built, but it was small and unable to handle the immensity of Minnesota's
central government. In 1896, Minnesotans decided they needed an architecturally
impressive state capitol building that would rival any other capitol building in the
world. They decided the best template from which to work would be Saint Peter's
Basilica in Vatican City.

The construction of the building was completed in 1905, and to this day it hosts the second-largest unsupported dome in the world, after Saint Peter's Basilica after which the dome was modeled. Throughout its history, political careers have been built and destroyed within these walls. Important decisions, affecting everyone in the state, originated here as well. It is no wonder this place is haunted, being an epicenter for artistic and architectural design and careers, and an epicenter for political decision-making.

ghost story

Early Minnesotan political figures still walk these hallways. People see men in 19th-century or early 20th-century clothing walking through the corridors of the building, especially at night. These figures are sometimes transparent and other times appear completely real until they disappear through a wall or simply vanish into thin air. These figures are seen throughout the building and mostly appear in remote areas when there is no one else around.

Most of the paranormal activity within the building seems to be concentrated on the second floor. Extreme cold spots are often reported in unusual locations—places where there couldn't be a draft from a poorly insulated window and nowhere near an air conditioning vent. Strange sounds also are reported from the second floor. Footsteps echo down the hallways although there is no one moving. Strange moans and other indecipherable vocal sounds are also reported here quite often.

Perhaps the most haunted place within the entire building is Room 217, which was once a judge's office in the early days of the capitol. People often feel uncomfortable in the room and sometimes the door to the room slams closed and locks while people are inside, trapping them in the room for several terrifying moments.

visiting

This building is open to the public every day of the year except for holidays. Monday through Friday, it is open from 8:30 a.m.–5 p.m. Saturday it is open from 10 a.m.–3 p.m., and Sunday it is open from 1–4 p.m. Every 45 minutes, free tours are offered of the capitol building, which cover the building's history and art. The only times you would be able to explore the capitol building in an attempt to search for ghosts would be during these hours.

SAINT ODILIA CHURCH AND SCHOOL

3495 North Victoria Street, Shoreview, Minnesota 55126

directions

From Minneapois, take I-35W North for about 8.5 miles to exit 27A, the I-694 East exit. Follow I-694 for about 3 miles to exit 43B, the Victoria Street exit. At the end of the exit ramp, turn right. Saint Odilia Church and School will be on your right about a half mile down the road.

history

The history of the Saint Odilia Church and School is by no means long. It wasn't until 1960 that the parish itself was founded in the suburbs of the booming Twin Cities metropolises. People living in the suburbs at that time not only needed a Catholic church at which to worship, but their children needed a Catholic school where they could learn.

The parish decided to build the school first, which was completed in 1962. The church followed several years later. During the early years of the school, it was staffed almost entirely with nuns as teachers. The nuns were from an order in Iowa, and many of them lived inside of the school, sleeping in classrooms. Eventually, another order of nuns took over teaching responsibilities, and several of those nuns teach at the school today. No one actually lives inside the school any more, but perhaps the spirits of those nuns who lived and worked in the building for so many years have stayed behind to make sure the students are being good.

ghost story

The ghost here seems to exist as either a warning or an omen. The paranormal activity always seems to precede some kind of unfortunate occurrence in either the church or the school. There is not one place where the activity occurs, but it seems to happen uniformly throughout the buildings.

For no earthly reason, the lights flicker in one of the rooms. There is no reason the lights would flicker, and it is almost as if a teacher is flashing the lights on and off to get a class's attention. Whenever this flickering occurs, something happens. Students have fallen off their chairs and broken their arms. People have had seizures and gotten into accidents throughout the school. Perhaps the nuns who spent so much time in the building are able to see the accident about to happen and flash the lights to try to prevent disaster.

visiting

The school is a grade school and closed to the public. To enter the school to try to experience the ominous flashing lights, you either have to be a student or an employee at the school. The church, though, is open for services during the weekend and welcomes anyone who wants to enter to worship. The flashing lights have been reported in the church too, so for the public to experience this ghost, they would have to visit the church during one of its services.

SOUTH ST. PAUL LIBRARY

106 Third Avenue N, South St. Paul, Minnesota 55075

directions

From downtown St. Paul, take Concord Street N across the river for about 3 miles until you reach Grand Avenue W. The road will curve to your left and change its name to Third Avenue. Follow Third Avenue for less than a block, and the library will be on your left.

history

This building has been around since 1927 and has been the central library in South St. Paul since that time. Throughout these 85 years of operation, countless people have spent countless hours within its walls. Whether it was a place to relax in quiet solitude or a place to learn or research for school or work, this place has become a hangout for those who are living as well as those who have passed.

ghost story

Many strange things are reported to have occurred within this building. Librarians and patrons alike have reported their fair share of ghostly happenings within these walls. Typically, the paranormal activity consists of sounds. Footsteps echo through the building, even when it is supposedly empty or when there is no one moving about. Others have actually heard voices within the building. Once a librarian was gossiping when suddenly a male voice said, "I can hear that." There was no one nearby who could have spoken those words. Most of the sounds occur in either the upstairs area or the basement. Both of these areas are open to the public. The upstairs houses the children's library while the basement is an area set up for teens.

A paranormal group investigated the building and determined that a small boy haunts the upper level. Although they didn't actually see the boy, they were able to communicate with him using dowsing rods. In addition to these sounds and the boy who may haunt the upstairs area, people often report feelings of unease within the building. Perhaps these feelings occur as they walk through a spirit of someone who had passed long ago but who still walks through this building as if they are still alive.

visiting

You can enter the building during regular business hours to search for ghosts. The library opens Monday through Friday at 9 a.m. On Monday and Thursday it is open until 8 p.m., and the rest of the week it is open until 6 p.m. On Saturday it is open from 10 a.m.–4 p.m., and on Sunday they are closed.

This is an operating library, so you still need to be quiet as you search the building for any kind of paranormal activity. They are proud of their ghosts, though, having invited paranormal groups into the building and approving authors to write paranormal articles about the library in the local papers. If you are respectful to the patrons, workers, and ghosts, you will have no trouble exploring this haunted location.

ST ANTHONY MAIN

219 Main Street SE, Minneapolis, Minnesota 55414

directions

St. Anthony Main is in the heart of downtown Minneapolis on the northeast side of the river across from Phillip W. Pillsbury Park. Take MN-65 across the river and turn right onto SE Second Street. Take the first right onto SE Third Avenue and then another right onto Main Street. St Anthony Main is on your right.

history

Across the street from St. Anthony Main was a small island in the Mississippi River called Spirit Island. The island was an important spiritual place for the Native Americans but was eventually overtaken by the Mississippi River. It currently sits underwater. Some say the Dakotas blamed the European settlers for what happened to their island. Some say that as the Europeans started building one of the first riverfront buildings in the town of St. Anthony across the river from Minneapolis, a building currently a part of St. Anthony Main, the Dakota placed a curse on the building. Shortly after it was completed, the wooden building burned to the ground. When it was rebuilt with stone, a train crashed into it and destroyed it. In addition, a series of untimely deaths occurred in the building.

St. Anthony Main was originally a series of buildings in St. Anthony in the 1850s, along First Street on the Mississippi River. Union soldiers occupied the buildings during the Civil War, but by the 1870s the area consisted mostly of factories. During this time, many of these factories employed small children. Children were able to work cheaper than adults, and the children could do things that larger men were unable to do. They were treated poorly, though. Some died in the factories or in the surrounding alleys from neglect or accidents. During renovations in the 20th century, tombs that contained small children were discovered on the property.

In the 1970s, the area was transformed from the industrial area that it had been for so many years to the tourist location that it is today. Souvenir shops and restaurants moved into the buildings. Eventually, the area consisted of condos and a movie theater. During the 20th century, more deaths occurred in the structure. Several homeless people died in the building. A couple of homeless people were found frozen to death, while another caught fire in an accident and burned to death. Still another man hung himself on the second floor of the building.

ghost story

Many ghosts haunt this building. Union soldiers have been seen lurking in this building's many stores and hallways. People often see children running around through all parts of the building as well—perhaps remnants of those factory children who were treated so poorly here in the past.

People report strange feelings when walking through the building. They feel uncomfortable or as if they are being watched. Sometimes, they actually get touched or scratched. Typically, when people are scratched by some unseen force, it occurs in the basement. A "Bad Man" who is rumored to haunt the basement may be the force behind these scratches. The second floor is haunted by a womanizer who makes himself known to women by touching them or talking to them.

Strange voices, which have no source, are heard throughout the building. No one else is present when these voices are heard. Electrical equipment reacts strangely as well. Batteries drain quickly and unexpectedly.

visiting

The stores and restaurants at St. Anthony Main are open to the public at a variety of hours during the day and night. Probably your best bet for finding the ghosts at St. Anthony Main is by taking their ghost tour, which runs Friday and Saturday nights at 7, 9, and 11 p.m. They provide you with EMF meters, dowsing rods, and flashlights as you commence your ghost hunting for the evening.

ST. OLAF COLLEGE

1520 St. Olaf Avenue, Northfield, Minnesota 55057

directions

From downtown Minneapolis or St. Paul, take I-35 South for about 35 miles to exit 69, towards Northfield. At the end of the exit, turn left onto MN-19 and follow that road for about 5.5 miles. After about 5.5 miles, the entrance to the campus will be on your left.

history

St. Olaf has been around for a very long time and has been a central educational establishment not only for Minnesota but for the entire country. Nine Rhodes Scholars have attended St. Olaf, and the school has one of the largest percentages of students in the world who go on to get doctorate degrees.

The college was founded in 1874 by Norwegian immigrants who wanted an educational institution that would suit their needs. It was named after Olaf II, the patron saint of Norway. Perhaps all those students and faculty who studied and taught here throughout the years have left a lasting impression upon the campus.

ghost story

This school seems to be absolutely infested with ghosts. We are not able to relay all the ghost stories that have been reported here in the limited space we have available, so let's focus on only the most famous ghosts that walk this campus.

At Melby Hall, the oldest hall currently standing at the school, people encounter two ghosts. One of these ghosts is a man and the other a woman, and they are dressed in late 19th-century clothing. This couple never seems to interact with the living. They are seen throughout the building, especially in the stairwells, before mysteriously fading away to nothingness.

At the Kelsey Theater, the ghost of a woman has been encountered several times. She is often seen and heard playing piano in the building before vanishing. She seems to be a benevolent ghost. Besides playing beautiful music on the piano, she has been known to warn those on stage of possible danger. One story tells of an actor about to back into the orchestra pit but was warned from behind by a disembodied voice.

At Hilleboe Hall, students hear children and music playing and are unable to locate the source of these sounds. Faucets suddenly turn on throughout the building for no reason. Children's handprints appear in condensation on the exterior of the third-floor windows.

The most famous ghost of the school, though, is that of a student in a red hat. Legend says the boy died unexpectedly off campus while he was a student at the college. He has apparently come back in an attempt to finish his education. The apparition is seen throughout campus, especially at night, and sometimes he is seen with a dog. The boy is seen most often in the vicinity of Thorson Hall. Some suggest this is the building where he lived when he actually attended the school.

visiting

The residence halls on campus are off limits to everyone except those who live there and their friends and family. As an outsider looking for ghosts, you are unfortunately unable to enter these dorms. The Kelsey Theater is open to the public for performances, though, so you do have a chance to encounter the ghost here, although she typically only appears when the building is mostly empty.

Your best chance for finding ghosts here is to simply wander aimlessly around the grounds of this beautiful campus. The most famous and prolific ghost, the boy in the red hat, is seen everywhere on campus, including the exterior areas.

ST. PAUL CITY HALL-RAMSEY COUNTY COURTHOUSE

15 West Kellogg Boulevard, St. Paul, Minnesota 55102

directions

This building is in the heart of downtown St. Paul on Kellogg Boulevard, just a block north of the Mississippi River. The building is a 21-story structure that sits on Kellogg Boulevard between Wabasha Street and St. Peter Street.

history

Built in 1931, the Saint Paul City Hall and Ramsey County Courthouse building houses the city's government and legal system. The most distinguishing facet of this building is the architecture itself. The 21-story exterior of the building appears stark and plain in the art deco style of the time. This almost plain exterior is contrasted by the interior of the building, where every door handle and light fixture is reminiscent of the art deco design of the 1925 Paris World's Fair.

The building was constructed during the heart of the Great Depression, when stress and suicide abounded throughout the country as fortunes were lost and people had to struggle to feed their families. Perhaps some of this depressing and tragic energy has imbedded itself into the walls of this building, or perhaps some of those who were convicted in the courthouse have returned to the place where they were last free.

ghost story

The most commonly reported ghosts here at the city hall and courthouse are apparitions, which do not appear to be the same person again and again, but instead it appears that various apparitions roam the building. The only thing that is common to these apparitions is they seem to be dressed in clothing from the 1920s or 1930s. These apparitions appear by walking through a wall and vanish as they walk through a wall on the other side of the room. They seem to have no sense of their surroundings and seem to be oblivious to the fact that there is a building here at all.

Late at night, security officers and custodians have often reported hearing strange sounds and voices echoing throughout the halls. Many times, these sounds are investigated by those working there, but one time security was so certain someone had broken into the building that they called the police to investigate. The police brought a K-9 unit to help find the intruder, but as they approached the front doors of the building, the dogs refused to enter. No one was found inside.

visiting

It is possible to tour the building and perhaps encounter one of the apparitions. Self-guided tours are available Monday through Friday from 8 a.m.–4:30 p.m. and can take between a half hour and two hours, depending on what you want to see. Even if you do not happen across one of the ghosts in the building, a tour of the building's beautiful interior is well worth your time and is completely free.

ST. THOMAS COLLEGE AND THE LEGEND OF THE 13 GRAVES

63 South Mississippi River Boulevard, St Paul,
Minnesota 55105

directions

From downtown St. Paul, take I-94 West for about 3 miles to exit 238, the Snelling Avenue exit. Turn left onto Snelling Avenue North and follow it for about a mile and then turn right onto Grand Avenue. Follow Grand Avenue for another mile, then turn right onto Cleveland Avenue South. Turn left onto Summit Avenue. Follow it to Mississippi River Boulevard and then turn left. There will be an entrance to the St. Paul Seminary School of Divinity on your left. After finding a place to park, follow a trail to the woods behind the Archbishop Ireland Memorial Library. This will take you to a grotto. The path to the 13 stone crosses follows the path of a ravine away from the grotto towards the Mississippi River and underneath the Mississippi River Boulevard bridge.

history

According to the legends, a priest ran a church near where St. Thomas College is today. One day he went crazy and raped the 12 nuns who worked with him at the church. The nuns didn't tell anyone and continued to work beside him at the church. But the priest couldn't live with the fact that he had to face his victims every day. One by one he killed the nuns and buried them in a ravine leading down towards the Mississippi River. When all 12 of the nuns were dead, he walked along the line of graves and killed himself. Today, there are 13 stone crosses lining the ravine where the priest buried his victims and killed himself.

While this story seems like the perfect beginning to a spooky ghost story, unfortunately for us ghost enthusiasts, it's not true. There are stone crosses that line the ravine down to the Mississippi River, but these stone crosses actually aren't graves at all: they're prayer stations that symbolize the stations of the cross. The stations of the cross are written in Latin on the base of the crosses. Some of the stations are missing or misplaced and difficult to find, which is why there are typically only a maximum of 13 crosses despite there being 14 actual stations of the cross. The line of crosses ends at the grotto.

ghost story

While the story of the murderous priest isn't true, there are still many people who claim to have experienced strange things along the path of these 13 crosses. The most often repeated phenomenon in this secluded stretch of stone crosses involves counting the crosses themselves. First of all, it is considered bad luck to count the crosses as you walk along the path. Those who do often claim to encounter some sort of calamity in their lives shortly thereafter. Also, if the crosses are counted multiple times, people often count a different number of crosses, suggesting that the actual number of crosses somehow changed between the first and second counts.

Beyond these strange stories involving the counting of the crosses, people also report intangible feelings of discomfort when they are in this area. Some visitors feel unwelcome or as though they are being watched as they traverse the trail. Others have heard screams or a man sobbing. The source of these sounds is never found.

visiting

This area is on the campus of the University of St. Thomas, so it is private property. If you are a student at the university, you should have no problem going at any time, but if you are not a student there, it is probably best to stick to daylight hours. This works best for a couple of different reasons. It isn't incredibly easy to find, especially at night, and it is incredibly dark on the path, so it would be much easier to find the crosses during the day. Incidentally, we counted eight crosses.

WASHINGTON AVENUE BRIDGE

MN-122 East and River Road East, Minneapolis,
Minnesota 55455

directions

From downtown Minneapolis, take South Fourth Street towards the south side of the city. Fourth Street will change its name to MN-122 and take you directly onto the University of Minnesota campus. At one point, a bridge crosses the Mississippi River, connecting the two different halves of the campus. While MN-122 takes you across this bridge, the haunted part is the pedestrian walkway on the upper deck of the bridge.

history

This bridge is actually the second bridge to span the Mississippi River and connect the campus of the University of Minnesota. The first bridge was built in 1884 and carried only foot traffic for the first six years of its existence. In 1890, it allowed streetcars and continued to carry both pedestrians and cars across the river until 1965, when the current bridge was built across the span slightly downstream from the original bridge. The new bridge again allowed for both pedestrian and vehicular traffic, but this bridge completely separated the two. The lower deck is reserved for cars while the upper deck is used by pedestrians. In the 1970s, an enclosure was built in the middle of the upper deck to help shield pedestrians from the oppressive cold that enveloped the bridge in the winter.

Throughout its history, the bridge has been the site of many tragedies. College is a very stressful time, and many college students are not able to handle the stress at times. Since the bridge is open throughout the night, it has become a place where depressed college students sometimes go with the intent of ending their own lives. Many suicides have occurred on the bridge as these college students throw themselves off into the icy waters below.

ghost story

The many suicides that have occurred on this bridge are blamed for the ghostly activity that currently haunts the span. Most of the time, the ghostly activity is experienced by those people who walk across the bridge late at night. These people often get the sensation they are being followed and sometimes hear footsteps following them across the bridge. These footsteps occur most prevalently in the tunnel area on the pedestrian deck of the bridge. People hear the footsteps behind them and then turn around and find no one else is in the tunnel. When they start walking again, the footsteps again start to follow them.

Another strange occurrence that happens upon the bridge is that the flags hanging from the bridge are ripped from the flag poles. The wind that is usually blowing across the bridge is not strong enough to cause any damage to the flags, but they are, from time to time, ripped. For a while, authorities assumed vandals had been messing with the flags, but when security cameras were installed on the bridge, it was discovered the flags were being torn by some other unseen force.

visiting

Luckily for those of us who are there to look for ghosts, the bridge is open throughout the night. The security cameras allow for a significant amount of safety, so you don't have to worry about being robbed on the bridge.

The best time to look for ghosts is late at night when no one else is on the bridge. The phantom footsteps occur most frequently inside the tunnel area of the pedestrian walking deck.

WILLOW LANE ELEMENTARY SCHOOL

3375 Willow Avenue, White Bear Lake, Minnesota 55110

directions

From St. Paul, take I-35E North for about 4 miles to exit 111A towards Stillwater. Follow MN-36 East for almost 2 miles to US-61 North. Follow US-61 North for 3 more miles and then turn right onto County Road E East. After about a half mile, turn right onto Linden Avenue. Linden changes its name to Willow Avenue. The elementary school will be on your right.

history

Willow Lane Elementary was built on swampland in the town of White Bear Lake. It was conceptualized as an elementary school and has continued to be one since it was built.

At least one of the haunts here at this school can be traced back to something that happened outside of the school itself. In fact, the only connection this event has to the school is that the child involved was a student at the school at the time. Many of the details of the crime are unclear, but this student was brutally murdered.

ghost story

The first ghost story at the elementary school is quite strange, and many of the students at the school who know about the ghost attribute it to the boy who was murdered. According to the rumors amongst the students, there is only one way to encounter this particular ghost within the school. You need to go into the downstairs boy's restroom on the last day of school and turn off the lights. Then you need to snap a picture. The ghost of the boy who was murdered will reputedly turn up in this picture.

While this first ghost story is somewhat strange and seems very much like an urban legend, there are other ghosts that supposedly haunt the grounds near the school. The swamplands and woods adjacent to the school are supposedly haunted by some menacing shadow figures. These shadow figures cannot leave the swamplands, but they supposedly attack anyone who enters their domain, causing intense fear and sometimes inexplicable scratches across the victim's body.

visiting

While the ghost of the murdered boy is next to impossible to try to encounter (unless, of course, you're a student at the school), the other ghosts are a little easier for an outsider to investigate. The school grounds themselves are off limits to outsiders, but the swampy area just to the south of the school is explorable, and this is what the menacing shadow figures protect. Besides any usual precautions you may take upon entering a wild swampland like this, watch out for those shadow people. They may bite.

APPENDIX I:
CHAPTERS ORGANIZED GEOGRAPHICALLY

ST. PAUL
St. Paul Cathedral
Minnesota State Capitol
Landmark Center
Saint Paul Hotel
Fitzgerald Theater
Oakland Cemetery
St. Paul City Hall-Ramsey County
    Courthouse
Forepaugh's Restaurant
Swede Hollow Park
Indian Mounds Park
Wabasha Street Caves
Padelford Packet Boat Company
Seltz' Point at Lake Como
Bluff Park
Mounds Theater
Hamline University Drew Hall
Hamline University
    Old Main Building
Marian Center
The Moonshine Saloon
St Thomas College and the Legend of
    the 13 Graves
Fort Snelling
Lilydale Park
South St. Paul Library
Hillcrest Recreation Center
Gibbs Farmhouse Museum

NORTH OF ST. PAUL
Roseville
Memorial Pet Cemetery
Shoreview
Saint Odilia Church and School
Linwood
County Highway 22 in Linwood

NORTHEAST OF ST. PAUL
White Bear Lake
Willow Lane Elementary School
Mahtomedi
Jessie Tomme Salon
Forest Lake
Carlos Avery State Wildlife
    Management Area
Taylors Falls
The Old Jail Bed and Breakfast

SOUTH OF ST. PAUL
Mendota Heights
Lebanon Hills Regional Park
Northfield
St. Olaf College
Dennison
Vang Lutheran Church

SOUTHEAST OF ST. PAUL
Grey Cloud Island
Grey Cloud Island
Grey Cloud Island Cemetery
Cottage Grove
Cottage Grove Historical Cemetery
Dead Man's Pond
Hastings
The Busted Nut
The Onion Grille
LeDuc Mansion
Ignatius Donnelly's Nininger City
    Home Site
Hastings State Asylum Cemetery
Red Wing
St. James Hotel

EAST OF ST. PAUL
Maplewood
Ramsey County Poor Farm Cemetery
Lake Elmo
Monastery at DeMontreville
Stillwater
Warden's House Museum
Water Street Inn
Arcola Trail Bridge
Wisconsin
Mabel Tainter Theater
East Immanuel Lutheran Church

MINNEAPOLIS
Minneapolis City Hall
The Soap Factory
St. Anthony Main
First Avenue Night Club
Washington Avenue Bridge
Minneapolis College of Art and Design
Minneapolis Institute of the Arts
Minneapolis Pioneers and Soldiers
    Cemetery
Lakewood Cemetery Mausoleum
Minnesota State Fairgrounds

NORTH OF MINNEAPOLIS
St. Anthony
Dairy Queen
Columbia Heights
Pizza Hut
Isanti
Oxlip Evangelical Free Church

NORTHWEST OF
MINNEAPOLIS
Brooklyn Park
AMF Earle Brown Bowl
Schmitt Music
Anoka
Anoka County Historical Society
Anoka City Hall
Anoka-Metro Regional Treatment
    Center
Artique, Inc.
Antiques on Main
Billy's Bar & Grill
Party Papers
Buffalo
Sturges Park
St Cloud
Skatin' Place

SOUTH OF MINNEAPOLIS
Richfield
Adam's Hill Park
Bloomington
Mall of America
Doubletree by Hilton Hotel
Burnsville
Burnsville Center
Alimagnet Park Trails
Apple Valley
Falcon Ridge Middle School
Dead Man's Hill
Owatonna
Minnesota State Public School
 Orphanage Museum

SOUTHWEST OF MINNEAPOLIS
Edina
Braemar Golf Course
Shakopee
Shakopee Memorial Park
Calvary Cemetery

Chaska
The Peacock Inn
Mill House Gallery
Carver
Carver Country Flowers and Gifts
Jordan
Johnson Memorial Drive
Montgomery
Montgomery National Golf Club
St Peter
Green Lawn Cemetery

WEST OF MINNEAPOLIS
Plymouth
Holy Name Cemetery
Long Lake
Holbrook Park
Long Lake (Union) Cemetery
Delano
Fountain Lake
Lake Rebecca Park Reserve
Plato
Ferguson Cemetery

APPENDIX II:

DAYTRIPPING (or in this case, NIGHTTRIPPING)

THE PARANORMAL PUB CRAWL
The best spirits in town!

1ST STOP: First Avenue Night Club

2ND STOP: St. Anthony Main

3RD STOP: Forepaugh's Restaurant

4TH STOP: Moonshine Saloon

5TH STOP: Busted Nut

6TH STOP: Onion Grille

7th Stop: Billy's Bar & Grill

(Remember, do not drive drunk. This city has enough ghosts; we don't need you making any more.)

SPEND A WEEK SLEEPING AROUND
Make sure you bring protection. . . .

SUNDAY: Peacock Inn Bed & Breakfast

MONDAY: Doubletree Hilton Hotel

TUESDAY: The Old Jail Bed & Breakfast

WEDNESDAY: Water Street Inn

THURSDAY: St. James Hotel

FRIDAY: St. Paul Hotel

SATURDAY: pitch a tent and spend the night in Bluff Park

THE LAND OF 10,000 GHOSTS...ER...LAKES, I MEAN
You won't need your wet suit and scuba supplies, just an EMF meter and a thermal camera. . . .

1ST STOP: Start simple at the small (and mostly empty) Dead Man's Pond

2ND STOP: look for a real-life gangster at Lake Como

3RD STOP: walk the trails surrounding Lake Alimagnet

4TH STOP: don't let the man on the bench fool you at Lake Rebecca Park

5TH STOP: listen for the woman splashing around in Fountain Lake

6TH STOP: look across the lake towards Long Lake Cemetery

ROAD TRIP!

Buckle up, watch out for pedestrians. . . .

1ST STOP: Drive your car by Calvary Cemetery and hope it doesn't die

2ND STOP: Drive past the Demontreville Monastery but look out for monks

3RD STOP: Look for strange, bloody women along County Road 22 in Linwood

4TH STOP: and then look for shadow figures along Johnson Memorial Drive

5TH STOP: end by crossing the Mississippi River over the Washington Bridge

THE MINNESOTA UNDERGROUND GHOST TOURS

Sometimes what you see on the surface is a tiny fraction of the haunting. . . .

1ST STOP: look for gangsters in the Wabasha Street Caves

2ND STOP: explore the basement at St. Anthony Main

3RD STOP: and the suicide tunnels at the Anoka State Hospital

4TH STOP: then spend the night in the haunted cave at the Old Jail Bed & Breakfast

APPENDIX III:

Places that Didn't Quite Make the Book

JAMES J. HILL HOUSE

Reason it didn't make the book: Possibly not haunted

Reason we wanted it in the book: Historic and creepy looking

THE STORY: This magnificent house was built in 1891 by one of the wealthiest men in St. Paul. He spared no expense in the creation of his mansion, and the building reflects this fact beautifully. The exterior utilized Richardsonian Romanesque architecture, which adds an incredible amount of creepiness to the place since this was the architectural style was used in many insane asylums built near the turn of the 20th century. The interior of the house looks like a haunted house. It is very reminiscent of the house from the film House on Haunted Hill or one of many episodes of Scooby Doo. Much of the stone work and interior sculpture and symbols have deeper occult meanings as well. Everything about this house screams ghosts.

As soon as I saw pictures of the house, I wanted it in the book. I went so far as to write the chapter. I wrote the history, the directions, and how to visit the place. The only thing left to do was to find out what ghosts resided inside. This is unfortunately where our search stopped. We were unable to uncover any stories about ghostly happenings in the building. We even talked to people who worked at the place. They were excited about the book, and they wanted ghosts in their house, but, unfortunately, there were none. Someone who has worked in the house for the last 25 years often worked after hours and was the only one in the building at night. He had never seen or heard anything strange while in the house. We even had someone take a tour through the house with an audio recorder in hopes of capturing a phantom voice that could prove there were ghosts here. There was nothing on the recording but the sounds of the tour itself.

If ever there were a house that should be haunted, this is it. Unfortunately, from what we can tell, it isn't.

HANNAH'S GRAVE

REASON IT DIDN'T MAKE THE BOOK: Can't find it

REASON WE WANTED IT IN THE BOOK: Original and strange story

THE STORY: We ran across the story of Hannah's Grave on the Internet and were immediately hooked because of its uniqueness. The story goes that a little girl named Hannah was playing near a windmill and somehow got her scarf caught on one of the spinning blades. Unable to free herself in time, the windmill lifted her from the ground by her neck and hung her to death. Not only was she killed in this freak accident, her family chose to bury her in front of the windmill that had killed her—not out of some macabre desire to remember her gruesome death but because of her love of the windmill during her life. According to the stories we read, her single grave still stands in front of the windmill.

The ghost stories say that strange things happen with your car if you drive by the windmill at night. Your car shuts off. Your headlights inexplicably blink on and off. Radio stations and cell phones suddenly lose signal. Also, the windmill sometimes starts to spin wildly on days without wind.

We wanted this story in the book, and this desire was heightened even more when we read online that people kept trying to find it but were unable. After all, that's what this book is about, helping people find these haunted places. All we had to go on was that it was in Waverly, Minnesota. We figured it would be easy—after all, how many windmills could there be in Waverly?

According to our search: 0. Eventually, we had to give up.

CHANHASSEN WATER TOWER

REASON IT DIDN'T MAKE THE BOOK: Not sure which water tower

REASON WE WANTED IT IN THE BOOK: Wanted to research the history and find out who the ghost is

THE STORY: Here is another instance where we figured it wouldn't be too hard to research a ghost story we'd heard. Apparently, a shadowy figure manifests itself on a water tower in Chanhassen. This shadowy figure not only manifests atop this tall water tower, but it actually dances there for several minutes before vanishing. No one knows anything about who this ghost might be. We figured this would be the perfect opportunity to search through recent records or talk to historical societies and find out who fell off the water tower to their death.

A couple of problems arose. First, no one we spoke to in Chanhassen had heard the story. Second, there are multiple water towers in Chanhassen. Not only were we not sure about the ghost any longer, but we also had no idea which water tower was supposedly haunted. The chapter couldn't make the cut.

CHANHASSEN DINNER THEATER

REASON IT DIDN'T MAKE THE BOOK: Management adamantly denies and discourages ghosts

REASON WE WANTED IT IN THE BOOK: Famous haunted location

THE STORY: According to the stories about the location, this theater was built over the site of a house that burnt to the ground. An unlucky woman was unable to escape the fire and died in the disaster. Another death involved an actress who was killed by a car while bicycling home from the theater. Both of these women have supposedly been seen throughout the theater. At least that is how the stories go.

As we began researching this location, we were warned by many sources that, not only is this location not really haunted, but the management is strongly against being considered a haunted location. Both the Chanhassen Dinner Theater and the Carver County Historical Society say there are no reliable reports of any ghostly activity ever happening inside of the building. Respecting their wishes, we did no further research.

PIERCE MOTEL

REASON IT DIDN'T MAKE THE BOOK: It's currently a halfway house, so inaccessible

REASON WE WANTED IT IN THE BOOK: Creepy-looking location with a creepier history

THE STORY: We were immediately interested in this location after seeing photographs and hearing the history. The building was constructed in 1906 by a Dr. Kline and was called Kline Sanitarium. Dr. Kline used what were considered cutting-edge medical practices at the time. Today, these practices are not used and are considered mostly ineffective. People went here depending on the doctor's medical expertise to help them get better, but they were ultimately never helped at all.

Pictures fall off the walls. People take photographs where faces appear that weren't there at the time that the picture was taken. People are attacked by invisible assailants in the basement. All of these are makings of a very haunted place with some good ghost stories. We had everything we needed for the chapter— a detailed history, ghost stories, and we knew where it was.

Then the problem arose. The Pierce Motel property consists of a couple of different buildings. The Pierce Motel itself is actually a one-floor hotel that looks like it was built in the 1970s or 1980s. Next to the Pierce Motel is the former Kline Sanitarium, an incredibly creepy and historic-looking building. The problem is that the building from the ghost stories isn't a hotel at all—it's a halfway house for those dealing with drug and alcohol addiction. Essentially, the building is a private residence and inaccessible to ghost explorers. We had to cut it from the book.

APPENDIX IV
LOCATION CHECKLIST

LOCATION	Visited	Investigated	Found a Ghost
Adam's Hill Park			
Alimagnet Park Trails			
AMF Earle Brown Bowl			
Anoka City Hall			
Anoka County Historical Society			
Anoka-Metro Regional Treatment Center			
Antiques on Main			
Arcola Trail Bridge			
Artique, Inc			
Billy's Bar & Grill			
Bluff Park			
Braemar Golf Course			
Burnsville Center			
Busted Nut, The			
Calvary Cemetery			
Carlos Avery State Wildlife Management Area			
Carver Country Flowers and Gifts			
Cottage Grove Historical Cemetery			
County Highway 22 in Linwood			
Dairy Queen			
Dead Man's Hill			
Dead Man's Pond			
Doubletree by Hilton Hotel			
East Immanuel Lutheran Church			

LOCATION	Visited	Investigated	Found a Ghost
Falcon Ridge Middle School			
Ferguson Cemetery			
First Avenue Night Club			
Fitzgerald Theater			
Forepaugh's Restaurant			
Fort Snelling			
Fountain Lake			
Gibbs Farmhouse Museum			
Green Lawn Cemetery			
Grey Cloud Island			
Grey Cloud Island Cemetery			
Hamline University Drew Hall			
Hamline University Old Main Building			
Hastings State Asylum Cemetery			
Hillcrest Recreation Center			
Holbrook Park			
Holy Name Cemetery			
Ignatius Donnelly's Nininger City Home Site			
Indian Mounds Park			
Jessie Tomme Salon			
Johnson Memorial Drive			
Lake Rebecca Park Reserve			
Lakewood Cemetery Mausoleum			
Landmark Center			
Lebanon Hills Regional Park			
LeDuc Mansion			
Lilydale Park			

LOCATION	Visited	Investigated	Found a Ghost
Long Lake (Union) Cemetery			
Mabel Tainter Theater			
Mall of America			
Marian Center			
Memorial Pet Cemetery			
Mill House Gallery			
Minneapolis City Hall			
Minneapolis College of Art and Design			
Minneapolis Institute of the Arts			
Minneapolis Pioneers and Soldiers Cemetery			
Minnesota State Capitol			
Minnesota State Fairgrounds			
Minnesota State Public School Orphanage Museum			
Monastery at DeMontreville			
Montgomery National Golf Club			
Moonshine Saloon, The			
Mounds Theater			
Oakland Cemetery			
Old Jail Bed & Breakfast, The			
Onion Grille, The			
Oxlip Free Evangelical Church			
Padelford Packet Boat Company			
Party Papers			
Peacock Inn, The			
Pizza Hut			
Ramsey County Poor Farm Cemetery			

LOCATION	Visited	Investigated	Found a Ghost
Regal Cinemas Brooklyn Center			
Saint Odilia Church and School			
Saint Paul Hotel			
Schmitt Music			
Seltz' Point at Lake Como			
Shakopee Memorial Park			
Skatin' Place			
Soap Factory, The			
South St. Paul Library			
St. Anthony Main			
St. James Hotel			
St. Olaf College			
St. Paul Cathedral			
St. Paul City Hall-Ramsey County Courthouse			
St. Thomas College and the Legend of the 13 Graves			
Sturges Park			
Swede Hollow Park			
Vang Lutheran Church			
Wabasha Street Caves			
Warden's House Museum			
Washington Avenue Bridge			
Water Street Inn			
Willow Lane Elementary School			

ABOUT THE AUTHORS

JEFF MORRIS

THIS IS JEFF MORRIS'S FOURTH BOOK. His first two books, *Haunted Cincinnati and Southwest Ohio* and *Cincinnati Haunted Handbook*, were written about his hometown of Cincinnati, where he currently resides with his wife and two children. His third book is *Nashville Haunted Handbook*. Morris founded a ghost tour in Miamitown, Ohio, in 2006 and still runs it today.

GARETT MERK

THIS IS GARETT'S SECOND BOOK. He is the founder of Tri-State Paranormal and Oddities Observation Practitioners, a paranormal study group based in Cincinnati, Ohio. Having an interest in ghosts since 2004, Garett has combined his knowledge of science with his passion for travel and technology to learn about paranormal activities around the world.

DAIN CHARBONNEAU

DAIN PETER CHARBONNEAU currently resides in Minnesota, where he also grew up enjoying the outdoor activities of camping and fishing. He is the founder of the Twin Cities Paranormal Research Group, which investigates claims of paranormal activity and researches the history from which the tales of activity stem. Dain is an avid sports fan and enjoys competing in hockey, softball, and soccer on a recreational level. In an effort to improve his health, he has become enthusiastic about participating in running and bicycling events around the Twin Cities, having completed three marathons and countless other events to.

Printed in the USA
CPSIA information can be obtained
at www.ICGtesting.com
JSHW012025140824
68134JS00033B/2874